365 Daily Gifts of Joy

Sandra Wright

365 DAILY GIFTS OF JOY

A JOYFUL DEVOTIONAL FOR
EVERY DAY OF THE YEAR

Sandra Mansfield Wright

ISBN-13: 9781978481213
ISBN-10: 1978481217

DEDICATION

This book is dedicated to my daughters, Karen and Kristi, in thanks for their love, encouragement, and support for me always. They are truly my gifts from God! I am so very proud of the wonderful women they have become.

JANUARY 1

"... for the joy of the Lord is your strength."
-NEHEMIAH 8:10

Sometimes I don't feel very strong or joyful. How about you? Problems hit us all: life situations in our family, friends, at work, money, health, depression, death of a loved one. These things can pull and tug on our joy and on our last bit of strength. We may feel that we are sinking, going down, but we can pray, read God's Word, and find again our joy and strength.

Today is the beginning of a new year, a new beginning. Every morning, we are given the gift of a new beginning. It is up to us to choose the joy of the Lord as our strength for this new day. Let His joy be our strength today as we face our problems. He will help us if we ask.

Prayer: God, may Your joy be my strength right now-this new year, this new day, this new beginning. Thank you. Amen.

Prayers, Thoughts, Gifts of Joy Today:

January 2

"Now the God of hope fill you with all joy and peace in believing, that you may abound in hope, through the power of the Holy Ghost."

-Romans 15:13

Hope and joy. Oh, to have these, then we have everything! In this new year, may our life be filled with the precious gifts of hope and joy. What is the thing called hope? I believe to have hope is to dream and accept that there is more ahead of us, to not lose faith, to trust and pray believing.

And the joy is the unspeakable deep, abiding, bubbling-up feeling inside of us of happiness, peace, contentment, and blessing from God.Only God can give true hope, joy, and peace. Pray. Ask Him for these blessings today, and then believe as we receive these. Rest in Him.

Prayer: God of hope, fill me with all joy and peace this very moment. Thank You. Amen.

Prayers, Thoughts, Gifts of Joy Today:

January 3

"This is the day which the Lord hath made; we will rejoice and be glad in it."

-Psalm 118:24

Today, be glad for the gift of another day. Rejoice today—this is the day we have been given. Christians should be the happiest, most joyous people in the world. Smile. Let your light shine and bless others. Bless and be blessed!

The gift of a smile, a kind word, or a good deed will brighten our day as well as the day of those around us. When we are glad, it spreads to others.

Prayer: Lord, thank you for this day. Help me to be glad in it and to bless those around me. Thank You. Amen.

Prayers, Thoughts, Gifts of Joy Today:

JANUARY 4

"A merry heart doeth good like a medicine . . . ."
-PROVERBS 17:22

Have a merry heart today as we go about our day. How do we get a merry heart? Pray and ask God to give us this merry (joyful) heart, and then go on our way expecting the gift of joy and merriment.

Celebrate this day that God has given us, this life that is our gift. My husband, David's, favorite song was "What a Wonderful World" by Louis Armstrong. The words in this song are a blessing and a message in themselves. Today, see and notice the beauty of the world all around. God made it beautiful for us to enjoy.

Prayer: God, give to me a merry, joy-filled heart today, and open my eyes to see the wonderful world around me. Thank You. Amen.

Prayers, Thoughts, Gifts of Joy Today:

". . . my mouth shall praise thee with joyful lips."

-PSALM **63:5**

P raise the Lord today with joyful lips and with the words we speak. Praise others in our life with joy as well. Speak words of kindness and joy as we go on our way this day. Let only kind words come from our lips today. Make this our goal, our commitment. All will receive a blessing if we do this. If we wake with a bad attitude or with problems on our mind, we can take time now to rethink, to reset our attitude, and start again. We can always begin again with God's help. Ask Him to give joy-filled lips, heart, and mind to us. What we think on and dwell on we become, so dwell and think on good. Right now, this minute, we should flood our mind with praise and joy!

Prayer: Psalm 19:14 "Let the words of my mouth, and the meditations of my heart, be acceptable in Thy sight, O Lord, my strength, and my redeemer." Thank You, Lord. Amen.

Prayers, Thoughts, Gifts of Joy Today:

JANUARY 6

"In the world you shall have tribulation; but be of good cheer; I have overcome the world."
-JOHN 16:33

Everyone is having a problem or will have a problem sometime in their life. This is just part of being human. Some problems are fairly small, while others are so mountainous, we may feel they are too large for us to get over. This verse encourages us to "be of good cheer," to remain positive and have hope, because God is in control. He has overcome the world! No matter what is going on in our world, we can know that God cares about what we are going through and can help. Just ask. When I have been in deep despair and felt that I could not bear the heartbreak, I cried out to God and He got me through the pain. He did not remove me from the situation, but He did help me to live through it. Hold on, pray, believing in the One who can help.

Prayer: Today, right now, I bring my burdens to You, God, and leave them with You. Thank You. Amen.

Prayers, Thoughts, Gifts of Joy Today:

"Sing for joy. Sing unto the Lord a new song, sing unto the Lord, all the earth."

-PSALM 96:1

Sing for joy to the Lord our God! Lift up a voice of praise to Him this day. Worship Him with song; even if we don't think we sing well, do it anyway. Singing helps to lighten our load, it makes us happier, and God likes to hear us. I believe He does. There are songs that just speak to us—the words fit our situation and express how we are feeling. Sing them aloud. Feel the melody in your heart. Music is just good for the soul. When you feel down, put on some good music to listen to, light a fragrant candle, and feel your mood lift. This works. It really does.

Prayer: Lord, lift my spirit today. Help me to be more joyful and to share Your joy with others around me. Thank You. Amen.

Prayers, Thoughts, Gifts of Joy Today:

JANUARY 8

"These things have I spoken unto you, that my joy might remain in you, and that your joy might be full."

-JOHN 15:11

J esus wants us to be filled with joy. He says over and over in the Bible that He loves and cares for us and wants good for His children. Why do we fight against His will for us so often? Somewhere in us, there is a voice that tells us to go our own way, to do things our way, that we know best for ourselves. It doesn't really make sense, does it? This is the way it is, though. Sometimes it's hard to know God's will for us. We may pray and ask, but then our own will gets in the way. How do we know God's will? One way to know is to pray and ask, then read His Word. He is never going to lead us to anything that goes against His Word. We can use His Word—the Bible—as our measure. Our joy will be full if we are in His will.

Prayer: God, I want Your joy today. Lead me. Guide me. Give me Your wisdom. Thank You. Amen.

Prayers, Thoughts, Gifts of Joy Today:

January 9

"... I will trust and not be afraid; for the Lord
Jehovah is my strength and my song."
-Isaiah 12:2

Today, we may be in need of extra strength as we go through a trial or handle a burden. Trust in the Lord, and do not be afraid. He promises to be our strength and give us a song in our heart again. There were days in my life, after my husband's death, when I thought I would never be able to sing or smile again. I could hardly breathe when panic and despair would settle in on me. I would read this verse, and others like it, and call out to God to help me. He helped me one day at a time. It wasn't an immediate fix. The problem did not go away, but day by day, I was able to live through it, with God's strength. I went on God's strength. Some things we just have to turn over to God because we cannot bear them by ourselves.

Prayer: Heavenly Father, give me strength and a song today. Lift me up, and help me not to be afraid. Thank You. Amen.

Prayers, Thoughts, Gifts of Joy Today:

JANUARY 10

"Thou hast put gladness in my heart."

-PSALM 4:7

Let the Lord fill our heart with gladness today. When we smile and are glad, good things seem to flow to us. Gladness brings its own rewards. Go out our door this morning and make it one of our goals to be glad for the day. Every morning we have a choice—we can be glad or we can be sad. Why choose to be sad when gladness is so much more fun? The Lord has given us so much to be glad about. Just look around at the good things, the beautiful things. We can major on the good and beautiful or the bad. Majoring on the good will bring more goodness into our day. Think up! Think glad!

Prayer: Lord, put more gladness in my heart this day. Let me be up, going, and doing Your will in gladness. Thank You. Amen.

Prayers, Thoughts, Gifts of Joy Today:

"The Lord is my strength and song . . . ."

-EXODUS 15:2

Look to the Lord, not to others, for our strength and for our song. Hopefully, there are dear friends and loved ones in this world for us to count on. Sometimes friends and loved ones can let us down, hurt or disappoint us. God is always faithful and true. He will be there and be constant. We may pull away from Him, but He will never leave or forsake us. The Bible promises this. If we pull away, He is there to welcome us back when we return. The Lord will be there for us throughout life. He will be our strength, our rock on which we can depend.

Prayer: Lord, help me to look to You for my guidance. Be my strength and the song of my heart. Thank You. Amen.

Prayers, Thoughts, Gifts of Joy Today:

JANUARY 12

"Who shall separate us from the love of Christ? Shall tribulation, or distress, or persecution, or famine, or nakedness, or peril, or sword? . . . Nay, in all these things we are more than conquerors through him that loved us."

-ROMANS 8:35, 37

Keep on keeping on! Nothing can separate us from the love of Christ. Nothing! God will help us through every day—even the bad ones. He is there to help us make it through if we will call on Him. I just listened to a song entitled "Leave Them There." It talks about taking our burdens to Jesus and leaving them with Him. This song spoke to me today. We are to lay our cares, our burdens, our worries at Jesus' feet and leave them there. He wants to carry us through this life. No one and nothing can separate us from God's love.

Prayer: Lord, help me today to keep on keeping on. Show me Your love; let me conquer all my problems through You. Be very close by me through everything today. Thank You. Amen.

Prayers, Thoughts, Gifts of Joy Today:

JANUARY 13

"I will be glad and rejoice in thee: I will sing praise to Thy name, O thou most High."

-PSALM 9:2

Rejoice, sing, and be happy! This is what God wants for us today. We have a loving and good Heavenly Father, so we should be glad. Of all people, we, as Christians, should be the happiest. We have much to celebrate and be happy about. Our Father is God Almighty! We are the children of the King! Remember this and think on this today as we go through our day and think up thoughts. Bless and be blessed as we go about our daily work. Reach out to others in God's love. Remember, we are children of God, so act like we are. Remember to whom we belong.

Prayer: Heavenly Father, thank You for Your love and Your watch and care over me today. Let me be thankful, glad, and praise You in everything I do today. Thank You. Amen.

Prayers, Thoughts, Gifts of Joy Today:

JANUARY 14

". . . ask, and ye shall receive, that your joy may be full."

-JOHN 16:24

We are to pray and ask God for our desires, but know that if we are reading the Bible and praying, we will know that our desires will be in keeping with God's will. I feel that some may take this verse out of context and use it for a blanket, "Ask God for anything, and you will receive it." God answers our prayers, I truly believe. I have heard it said there are three answers: "yes, no, and wait." I have had my prayers answered by all of these at one time or another. We have to believe that God sees the big picture, knows the end of our story, and knows what we need and when we need it. Often, we may ask for things that are not in our best interest in the long run. God wants us to have joy—"That your joy may be full." He knows what we truly need to give us that full joy. Trust Him.

Prayer: Lord, help me to have the wisdom to know how to pray and ask. Thank You. Amen.

Prayers, Thoughts, Gifts of Joy Today:

JANUARY 15

"Rejoice evermore. Pray without ceasing. In everything give thanks; for this is the will of God in Christ Jesus concerning you."

-1 THESSALONIANS 5:16-18

Once again, God is telling us to rejoice and be happy. He also tells us to pray all the time. Be in an attitude of prayer as we go about our day where we can quickly and often call out to God to say, "Thank You, God. Help me, God. Be with them, God." Again, we are to recognize that God sees and knows what we need even before we know, and He has our best interest in mind. We are to thank Him in everything. Yes, everything. This may be hard to do because we may not like what has happened to us. He can and often does take something bad and turn it into something good for us. The bad thing may have been the consequence of our wrong choice or someone else's wrong decision. He can turn our wrong into right again. He does forgive, thank goodness. It may not be His first plan for us, but He can "turn our sorrow into joy."

Prayer: Thank You, God, for everything You have done for me. Amen.

Prayers, Thoughts, Gifts of Joy Today:

JANUARY 16

"Let all those that put their trust in thee rejoice: let them ever shout for joy, because thou defendest them; let them also that love thy name be joyful in thee."

-PSALM **5:11**

L et us put our trust in God, rejoice and shout for joy, and be happy! Our day, this day, is ours to enjoy. The good Lord gave us this day. What will we choose to do with this gift of a day? Let's make the most of it. Begin this day with prayer and good thoughts: thoughts of praise, thanksgiving, and joyfulness. Trust God. Shout for joy and be filled with the awe, the magnificence of the miracle of a new day. Hold up your head and go forward into the day ahead with a renewed sense of purpose and delight. We are God's child, and He has given us this new day!

Prayer: Thank you, God, for today, this day You have given me. I am thankful and appreciate all You give me. Let me use today wisely for Your glory. Thank You. Amen.

Prayers, Thoughts, Gifts of Joy Today:

JANUARY 17

"The fruit of the Spirit is love, joy, peace, long-suffering, gentleness, goodness, faith, meekness, temperance; against such there is no law."
-GALATIANS 5:22-23

The fruit of our lives, if we are a Christian, is to be these nine things. We may not bear these fruits continually, but we are to strive for them. God gives us these if we ask and work toward them, I believe. In Matthew 7:16 it says, "You shall know them by their fruits . . . ." This indicates that people can see our actions, our fruits, and know whether we are God's children. We should watch our actions—what we speak and what we do—so that we can represent God well today. I have failed sometimes. I am not perfect, but I strive to do right and ask forgiveness frequently when I fall short. God forgives and helps me to do better. Strive to bear good fruit.

Prayer: Lord, help me to have the fruits of the Spirit in my life today. Thank You. Amen.

Prayers, Thoughts, Gifts of Joy Today:

**". . . in thy presence is fullness of joy; at thy
right hand there are pleasures for evermore."**
-PSALM 16:11

Celebrate this day! Find joy in fullness! With God in our
life, we can have joy and be happy. This does not mean
we will not have problems in our life even after we become a
Christian. In this world, we will have troubles, but God has
promised to be with us through our troubles, to love us, to
hold us with his right hand, and to help us always. Do not
lose hope and joy, for He will be there. Keep praying. Keep
reading His Word. Keep believing. He will help us through.
I can personally testify to this. Even in our deepest despair,
He will be there for us and bring us through. Hold on. He is
there!

Prayer: Let me feel Your presence today and know You
are here with me, Lord. Give me Your joy! Thank you. Amen.

Prayers, Thoughts, Gifts of Joy Today:

"And the peace of God, which passeth all understanding, shall keep your hearts and minds
through Christ Jesus. Finally, brethren, whatsoever things are true, whatsoever things are
honest, whatsoever things are just, whatsoever
things are pure, whatsoever things are lovely,
whatsoever things are of good report; if there be
any virtue, and if there be any praise, think on
these things."

-PHILIPPIANS 4:7-8

Think on good as we go about our day today. Truth, honesty,
justice, purity, loveliness, goodness, virtuousness—things
that are good. Think on these. Fill our mind and heart with the
good, not the bad. Think up. Dwell on good and become a better person by doing so. Thinking on good will bring our heart
and life peace in this upside-down world. It will steady us. Our
soul will be refreshed and lighter.

Prayer: Dear God, You who refreshes and uplifts me, thank
You for being with me today. Give me eyes to see the beauty
and the good, give me ears to hear the good in the world
today, and let me be the good that others see and hear in
their world today. Thank You. Amen.

Prayers, Thoughts, Gifts of Joy Today:

January 20

"And he hath put a new song in my mouth, even praise unto our God: many shall see it, and fear, and shall trust in the Lord."

-PSALM 40:3

Praise to the Lord! Sing to the Lord today. When we are happy, sometimes we sing or hum, don't we? The Lord loves for us to be happy and to sing and dance. In Psalm, David, the writer, often writes about singing and dancing for joy to the Lord and playing instruments. When we are happy in the Lord, it shows, and others will see a difference in us, a difference from the world. Hopefully, this will lead others to Christ. Let our light and our joy shine so that others may see and trust in the Lord.

Prayer: Today, Lord, may I conduct myself in such a way as to lead others to You as their Savior and source of joy. Thank You. Amen.

Prayers, Thoughts, Gifts of Joy Today:

"Peace I leave with you, my peace I give unto you: not as the world giveth, give I unto you. Let not your heart be troubled, neither let it be afraid."

-JOHN 14:27

"Let not your heart," your life, "be troubled!" Rest in God's promises. Let Him give us His peace. Have confidence in Him. When we read the Bible, we find so many times that He says He will never leave us or forsake us. He will be with us through our troubles and problems and promises to raise us up. Have hope in God. Trust. Have faith. Draw strength from His Holy Word each day before we go out our door and face the problems of the day ahead. Know that He will get us through. Stand strong in this knowledge.

Prayer: Lord, give me Your peace, Your calm today. Take my troubled spirit and fear away. Let me feel peaceful, calm, and know You are with me through it all today. Thank You. Amen.

Prayers, Thoughts, Gifts of Joy Today:

"Be strong and of a good courage, fear not, nor be afraid of them: for the Lord thy God, he it is that doth go with thee; he will not fail thee, nor forsake thee."

-**DEUTERONOMY 31:6**

We know the one who can calm the storm today, don't we? God can! Last night, when I went to bed, a storm was predicted to hit our area during the night. Since my husband died, and I am living alone, the predictions of bad weather make me nervous and unsettled. I feel a little afraid. I prayed and asked God to keep me safe, and then I went off to sleep, feeling more secure. We can do this with any storm in our life, whether it be storms of doubt, trouble, or other turmoil. He can calm!

"You can't calm the storm so stop trying. What you can do is calm yourself."

-**ZIG ZIGLAR**

Prayer: Lord, give me courage and strength today to do all I have to do with Your confidence. Thank You. Amen.

Prayers, Thoughts, Gifts of Joy Today:

"I will lift up mine eyes unto the hills, from whence cometh my help. My help cometh from the Lord, which made heaven and earth."

-PSALM 121:1-2

My help comes from the Lord! Trust and have faith in Him. I read a quote from Barbara Johnson: "While sorrow looks back and worry looks around, faith looks up." Let us look up today and keep our eyes on Jesus, who helps us. Worry and sorrow won't help us, but faith will. An old song tells us to turn our eyes to Jesus. When we do this, the things of this earth—the worries, the troubles, the stress, the daily grind—will grow dim when compared with God's glory, mercy, and grace! He is bigger than our problems. Oh, yes!

Prayer: Let me look up in faith today, Lord. Let my sorrow and worry grow dim and fade away when I put my eyes on You. Let me trust in You, God, my help! Thank You. Amen.

Prayers, Thoughts, Gifts of Joy Today:

JANUARY 24

"The Lord is good, a stronghold in the day of trouble; and he knoweth them that trust in him."

-NAHUM 1:7

Our help, our stronghold, is the Lord! When we are in trouble and despair, we can call on Him to help us, to bring us out. We should call on Him every day, not just wait until trouble comes. If we pray and call on Him daily to walk with us, to give us wisdom and strength day to day, our burdens will be lighter, and we will be strong enough to bear them because we have His help constantly. Trust in the Lord. He is there—always ready to guide and to help because He loves and cares and knows us.

Prayer: Lord, help me look to You today for my help and strength! I trust in You! Give me wisdom in everything I do today. Thank You. Amen.

Prayers, Thoughts, Gifts of Joy Today:

"Ask, and it shall be given you; seek, and ye shall find; knock, and it shall be opened unto you. . . . If you then, being evil, know how to give good gifts to your children, how much more shall your Father, which is in heaven, give good things to them that ask him?"

-MATTHEW 7:7, 11

The Bible teaches us if we ask, we will receive good things from our Heavenly Father. In my opinion, and from studying the Bible, this is not a verse that means ask for a car and receive a car. The entire Bible deals with the best gifts for you—heart and soul gifts. If we are continually praying and yearning for God in our life, we will pray in the "right" spirit, with the "right" heart. We will ask for things that are in God's will and in our best interest. Oh, we may even ask for a car. We may need this, and it may not be a wrong prayer for us. God knows what we need and when we need it. Trust Him.

Prayer: Thank You, Lord, for being my Heavenly Father. Help me to ask for the right things for my life. Thank You for all You have given me and continue to give me. Amen.

Prayers, Thoughts, Gifts of Joy Today:

"Rejoice evermore. Pray without ceasing. In everything, give thanks: for this is the will of God in Christ Jesus concerning you."

-1 THESSALONIANS 5:16-18

Rejoice always and be glad today, this day the Lord has given us! It's easy to rejoice when things are going well and to give thanks for the good things, isn't it? But what about on days when we are ill, feel bad, have family, work, or friend problems, or have tragedy in our life and our hearts are broken? Can we praise God and rejoice on these days? I know it is hard, but when these verses say "rejoice evermore" and "pray without ceasing," this means to stay in an attitude of prayer and thanksgiving. Trust in our Lord. Keep on praying, even when we don't feel up to it; it is especially important then. When we don't understand "why," we have to keep on praying and trusting.

Prayer: I rejoice and am glad in this day You have given me, and thank You, Lord, for ALL You have done for me. Even on days that are hard, I feel Your blessings and give thanks because I put my trust and hope in You! Thank You. Amen.

Prayers, Thoughts, Gifts of Joy Today:

JANUARY 27

**". . . be strong and of a good courage; be not
afraid; neither be thou dismayed: for the Lord
thy God is with thee whithersoever thou goest."**
-JOSHUA 1:9

The Lord is with us no matter what is happening in our lives. He is there to help us, to support us, and to bring us through. He loves and cares because He made us. We are encouraged to be strong and courageous because our God is on our side. When we are afraid, we can call out to God to help. This verse goes on to say "do not be dismayed" (distressed, worried, or concerned) because God is with us wherever we go, whatever is going on. As Christians, we can have confidence, trust, and hope in our God! Be filled with His strength, His blessings today!

Prayer: Lord, help me to be strong and of good courage today. Let me not be dismayed, stressed, or worried. Let me put my trust in You with all my life, my decisions, my dreams, my future, and plans. Guide me today, O Lord. Thank You. Amen.

Prayers, Thoughts, Gifts of Joy Today:

". . . I will be with thee: I will not fail thee, nor forsake thee."

-JOSHUA 1:5

God says many times in the Bible that He will be with us and never leave us or forsake us. In this life, many may have been left or deserted by someone, but God will never do this. He will keep on being there for us, just a prayer away. When we need help with anything, we can call out to Him. The Bible is such an encouraging and uplifting book. Read it every day for strength and to help find great hope. I promise you will be blessed and find the strength to face every challenge in life. It will give us the strength and power to go on.

Prayer: Thank You, Lord, for always being there for me, even when I don't deserve Your love and when I doubt and question "why?" Thank You for this verse of assurance today, that You will always be there for me and never fail me or forsake me. Thank You. Amen.

Prayers, Thoughts, Gifts of Joy Today:

". . . to be spiritually minded is life and peace."
-ROMANS 8:6

Set your mind on things of God—good things. When we let our minds dwell on the bad and ugly things of life, we can become down, discouraged, and depressed. God's Spirit is one of love, beauty, life, and peace. Think on these and live fully. We have a new year ahead of us to think up and to do good. Go for it each day, afresh and anew, with celebration and excitement, God's love, hope, and peace. He will give us hope, a new hope every day. As Christians, we have a great hope above all others. Praise God!

Prayer: God of hope, fill me with Your Spirit today. Give me Your hope and peace. Set my mind on You. Thank You. Amen.

Prayers, Thoughts, Gifts of Joy Today:

JANUARY 30

"And we know that all things work together for good to them that love God, to them who are called according to his purpose."

-ROMANS 8:28

(All Things) work together for good. This is sometimes difficult to accept or understand, but this is what the Bible says. I know from my own life that things I have thought to be awful and painful at the time have, in the long run, turned out to have been good for me in many ways. These may not have been what I thought I wanted in my life, not my choice, but God turned bad into good for me. This does not mean God caused all the bad to happen. Bad things sometimes happen as a consequence of our actions or our choices—or often the choices or actions of others—but God can even turn the bad into good for us if we love Him and pray for His help in every area of our lives.

Prayer: Lord, help me this day to walk in Your way, to make wise and good choices, and when bad things happen to ask for Your help, and then trust You to work them out for the good. Thank You. Amen.

Prayers, Thoughts, Gifts of Joy Today:

JANUARY 31

"Take no thought then . . . for your heavenly Father knoweth that ye need all these things. But seek ye first the kingdom of God, and his righteousness, and all these things shall be added unto you. Take therefore no thought for the morrow: for the morrow shall take thought for the things of itself."

-MATTHEW **6:31-34**

Do not worry about tomorrow. Trust in our Heavenly Father. He knows what we need. Seek first God and His goodness for our life, and He will give us what we truly need. I don't know about you, but I spend a lot of time worrying and being anxious. There are so many scriptures in the Bible that tell us not to worry, not to fret, not to be anxious, and then encourage us to trust God, who loves us and cares. Then why do we worry? This worry thing must be a very real problem with us humans, since the scriptures address it so often. We need to listen, rest, and relax in our Savior.

Prayer: Let me rest, relax, and trust in You today, Lord. Let me stop worrying about tomorrow, but trust tomorrow to You. Thank You. Amen.

Prayers, Thoughts, Gifts of Joy Today:

FEBRUARY 1

"For thou hast made him most blessed for ever: thou hast made him exceeding glad with thy countenance."

-PSALM 21:6

E xceeding glad (joy)! God will give us joy in our hearts this day. Just ask for it. Think on God, have joy and gladness as we go through this new day, this new month—February, the month love is celebrated. Let us love in our hearts and pay close attention to those around us: at home, at work, at the stores, the cafes, on the street—everyone we meet throughout our day. Begin in the morning by asking God to help us show His love today to everyone we meet. Let's start with our family, those with whom we live, and then branch out as we leave our door. Love and be glad! We will be blessed as we bless others!

Prayer: Lord, thank You for putting gladness (joy) in my heart today. Let me bless and be blessed this day as I go about my day. Help me to love others. Thank You. Amen.

Prayers, Thoughts, Gifts of Joy Today:

FEBRUARY 2

"Rejoice in the Lord always: and again I say, Rejoice."

-**PHILIPPIANS 4:4**

Rejoice in the Lord! Celebrate this day the Lord has given us to enjoy. In everything, rejoice. God sends us joy, laughter, and fun. He made our body so it could smile and be happy. He gave us senses so we could see the beauty all around us, hear birdsong and laughter, touch the wonders of the earth, smell the flowers, and taste the delicious foods He gives us. For those who have lost one or more of these senses, He often gives extraordinary abilities in other areas. Rejoice in what we do have, and be thankful always and in everything.

Prayer: Lord, thank You for all You have given me. Let me rejoice and be glad in this day and give You the praise always. Thank You. Amen.

Prayers, Thoughts, Gifts of Joy Today:

February 3

> "O come, let us sing unto the Lord; let us make a joyful noise to the rock of our salvation. Let us come before his presence with thanksgiving, and make a joyful noise unto him with psalms."
> -Psalm 95:1-2

Sing to the Lord! You may say, "I can't carry a tune," but the Bible says to "make a joyful noise," so sing anyway. When we sing, it lifts our spirit and makes us happier. Just go around the house, singing. Listen to praise songs and sing along. This very act will lighten us. I read that if you are down and sad, put on happy, uplifting music, turn on the lights, light some candles, and these things will help lift your spirits. I add to this, sing along with the music. Read some uplifting scriptures. Think up!

Prayer: Lord, I thank You today for Your love, mercy, and grace to me. I praise Your name. I sing unto You a glad song of joy and praise. Thank You for everything You have done. Amen.

Prayers, Thoughts, Gifts of Joy Today:

"For I the Lord thy God will hold thy right hand, saying unto thee, Fear not; I will help thee."

-ISAIAH 41:13

God promises to hold my right hand, protecting me, so I have no need to fear. Even though I know this and believe this, sometimes the fears and doubts come creeping in. This is one of those verses we should write on a card and tape to our mirror so we see it every morning as we begin our day. We should memorize this verse and say it over and over again. I used to hear the term "claim God's promise." This is one of His promises we should claim as especially for us, and then trust Him to hold our hand through whatever we are going through today. Claim this promise today and hold on to God's hand.

Prayer: Oh God, help me today! Hold my right hand, guide me, and keep me from falling or failing. You say "do not fear," so I won't. I put my faith and trust in You. Thank You. Amen.

Prayers, Thoughts, Gifts of Joy Today:

"I can do all things through Christ which strengtheneth me."

-PHILIPPIANS 4:13

With God, all things are possible. I pray to Him and put my faith and trust in Him, and then He will help me through every day. With His strength, I can make it. He is my encourager and the One who will keep me keeping on. We, as Christians, have a constant source of strength right there beside us all the time, even through our darkest hours. Turn to Him. Ask Him for help. Let Him help us through this time, whatever we are facing. We don't have to go through it alone. Find strength in Jesus Christ.

Prayer: Jesus, strengthen me, help me through this. Hold my hand. Thank You. Amen.

Prayers, Thoughts, Gifts of Joy Today:

FEBRUARY 6

"It is of the Lord's mercies that we are not consumed, because his compassions fail not. They
are new every morning: great is thy faithfulness.
The Lord is my portion, saith my soul; therefore
will I hope in him."

-LAMENTATIONS 3:22-24

I will hope in Him! His mercies are new every morning!
Thank goodness He doesn't give us what we deserve, but
gives us mercy, kindness, love, forgiveness, and grace. Every
morning, every new day, He gives us a new beginning. Each
day is a blessing from God to begin again, to start fresh with
Him. He is faithful to us. Let us be faithful to Him as we
live this new day. Pray to Him. Ask Him for forgiveness, ask
for His guidance, His strength, His hope in times of trouble,
worry, and fear. Let Him lift us up.

Prayer: Thank You, Lord, for Your mercy, forgiveness,
and grace. Thank You for giving me hope. Thank You for
this new morning. You are my portion, my strength, and my
help. Thank You. Amen.

Prayers, Thoughts, Gifts of Joy Today:

February 7

"Thou wilt keep him in perfect peace, whose mind is stayed on thee, because he trusteth in thee. Trust ye in the Lord forever: for in the Lord, Jehovah is everlasting strength."

-Isaiah 26:3-4

Trust in the Lord. He is the only one who can give you real peace, perfect peace. Even when things are falling apart, when we feel alone or defeated, the Lord can be our strength when we trust in Him. Trust. Hope. Believe. Pray. Ask. In this world, we will have sorrows and problems, but if we keep our eyes on Jesus, He will see us through. I believe this with my whole heart because I have experienced it personally. When our minds are focused on Jesus Christ, we will see more clearly the things that really matter.

Prayer: Lord, I pray for Your "perfect peace" in my life this moment and through this day. Let me think on You and trust You to get me through. Thank You. Amen.

Prayers, Thoughts, Gifts of Joy Today:

> ". . . you now therefore have sorrow: but I will see you again, and your heart shall rejoice, and your joy no man taketh from you."
>
> -JOHN 16:22

These were the words of Jesus to His disciples and to us. He said we would sometimes experience sorrow, but He would give us joy and rejoicing again. I lost my husband, David, in February 2015 and felt such sorrow and pain as I had never felt before. I thought I might never feel joy again. This is a verse that spoke to me, encouraged me, and helped me through a hard, dark time in my life. God gives us hope that we will see Him and our loved ones who have gone on before us. Jesus conquered death and the grave. Amen!

Prayer: Thank You, God, for giving me hope and joy in my life and keeping near to me through the times of sorrow. Thank You. Amen.

Prayers, Thoughts, Gifts of Joy Today:

FEBRUARY 9

"For I know the thoughts that I think toward you," saith the Lord, "thoughts of peace, and not of evil, to give you an expected end."

-JEREMIAH 29:11

God has good thoughts and plans for us. He loves us, cares, and wants us to have peace, joy, and happiness. He doesn't plan evil for us. Sometimes bad does come into our life. Sometimes it is due to our own or someone else's wrong choices and the consequences of these. Sometimes bad things happen to good people, and we don't know why and we may question why. In my own life, God has taken bad and eventually turned it into good for me. In life, bad things and problems do exist. Be strong and of good courage because God has a plan for you, and it isn't evil; it is for good.

Prayer: God, take this problem, this hurt, this worry and bring about good through it in my life. Help me deal with it as You would want and to bless You through it. Thank You. Amen.

Prayers, Thoughts, Gifts of Joy Today:

"Is any among you afflicted? Let him pray. Is any merry? Let him sing psalms. . . . The effectual fervent prayer of a righteous man availeth much."

-JAMES 5:13, 16

P ray. We are to pray about all things in our life. When we are happy, we are to sing songs of praise to God. Thank Him for the ability to pray, for the peace, hope, and calm of prayer. Prayer can soothe, comfort, calm, and drive away the storm and fear in our lives. Our God is still able to calm the storms. God hears us when we pray and sing praises to Him. I read once that He always answers prayer. He may answer "yes, no, or wait." Pray, and then ask for the best thing for yourself or others. Only God knows what's best for us, and He wants the best for us.

Prayer: Thank You, God, that You made a way for me to pray directly to You through Jesus Christ. I pray today for Your will to be done in my life. I can stop worrying when my life is in Your capable hands. Thank You. Amen.

Prayers, Thoughts, Gifts of Joy Today:

FEBRUARY 11

"O taste and see that the Lord is good: blessed is the man that trusteth in him."

-PSALM 34:8

The Lord is good to us, and we are blessed by Him. We should be aware of His love and care for us in every moment of our lives—and be thankful. Live in a state of thankfulness and awareness of His mercies and blessings. When we trust God with every part of our life, we will be open and aware of even more of His blessings. Sometimes we may have pain or problems, but as we learn to trust God, we can see that even what we, at the time, may perceive as bad things can become blessings. Trust God in everything!

Prayer: God, I trust You to bless and care for me in all things. Help me to see, really see, Your blessings in my life. Help me to bless You and be more thankful. Thank You. Amen.

Prayers, Thoughts, Gifts of Joy Today:

FEBRUARY 12

"And let the peace of God rule in your hearts, to which also ye are called in one body; and be ye thankful."

-COLOSSIANS 3:15

Allow God to give us His peace. Peace is the absence of fear. It is a calmness, even in the midst of strife. We can have peace—even when our world around us is shaken—if we pray and remain in His hands. When we trust God, we know He is watching over us in all things. Keep on trusting. Keep on believing. Keep on praying and thanking. Praise Him and be thankful for His help in times of trouble. Let His peace rule in our heart. Open up to His peace.

Prayer: God of peace, let me open my heart to You today. Take all the storms of worry, doubt, fear, strife, stress, sickness, loneliness, and heartache away, and give me Your calm, Your peace, and Your care in its place. Thank You, Lord. Amen.

Prayers, Thoughts, Gifts of Joy Today:

"Casting all your care upon him; for he careth for you."

-1 PETER 5:7

Put "ALL" our cares, our worries, and concerns on Him, because He loves us and wants to help us. Pray to God with trust, knowing He loves and cares. Sometimes this is hard for us to really grasp—to come to the realization that Almighty God cares for us and wants our best. We can give all our problems to Him every day and stop this constant worrying and stressing. "It sounds so simple, it just can't be true," we say. The Bible tells us over and over to trust God, to give Him our burdens and cares, to depend upon Him. So why don't we? Is it because we are giving control over to Him? Well, ultimately He is in control anyway, right? So do it now. Give it over.

Prayer: God, I give You control of my life this day, right now. I give You ALL my cares. Thank You for loving me. Amen.

Prayers, Thoughts, Gifts of Joy Today:

"I will love thee, O Lord, my strength."

-PSALM 18:1

Sometimes I don't feel very strong. How about you? But at these times, that's exactly when I need the Lord the most. I can call out to Him in my weakness and know that He will be my strength for me. I praise Him and love Him for this. What happens when we love the Lord? We trust Him. We put our faith and hope in Him. We put our life in His hands. We depend on Him to be beside us in life and help us make it through every day, every week, every month, and every year until the end of this life on earth, and then on to eternity in heaven. What a glorious hope!

Prayer: I love You, Lord, my strength! Thank You for Your hope within me, that I may face this day before me. You gave me this day, so let me use it well to love and help others and share Your love with all You place in my path today. Thank You. Amen.

Prayers, Thoughts, Gifts of Joy Today:

FEBRUARY 15

"Speak to yourselves in psalms and hymns and spiritual songs, singing and making melody in your heart to the Lord, giving thanks always for all things unto God and the Father in the name of our Lord Jesus Christ."

Make a melody in our heart to the Lord. Sing praises to Him. This will give life to our heart and make us feel good. Read the scriptures, hum a tune, pray, and offer up our praise and thanksgiving to the Lord. If we are down, sad, depressed, and low, these simple acts will lift our spirit. I promise. I know this for a fact. I have done it. Get the Bible out, turn on some music— music that will glorify God— then pray and listen.

Prayer: Thank You, God, for the blessing of music in my life; for song, for prayer, and praise. Thank You. Amen.

Prayers, Thoughts, Gifts of Joy Today:

FEBRUARY 16

"The righteous cry, and the Lord heareth, and delivers them out of all their troubles. The Lord is nigh unto them that are of a broken heart; and saveth such as be of a contrite spirit."

-PSALM 34:17-18

The scriptures tell us that God is near to us when we are broken, sad, and cry out to Him for help. He will bring us out and deliver us from our sorrow and troubles. The Bible doesn't promise us we will have no problems and troubles in life; problems are just a part of life. But the Bible does promise that He will be with us through life's troubles, help us, and deliver us from our troubles. As Christians, we are offered a God who cares for us, loves us, and gives us hope—a helper in times of need. He will be there when we call on Him, anytime and anywhere.

Prayer: Thank You, God, for being there for me today when I call on You to help me. You have been there for me so many times before, and I trust You that You will be there always. Thank You. Amen.

Prayers, Thoughts, Gifts of Joy Today:

"Beloved, let us love one another: for love is of God; and every one that loveth is born of God, and knoweth God. He that loveth not knoweth not God, for God is love. In this was manifested the love of God toward us, because that God sent his only begotten Son into the world, that we might live through him. Herein is love, not that we loved God, but that he loved us, and sent his Son to be the propitiation for our sins."

-1 JOHN 4:7-10

Remember this. Know this. God loves us. He cares about us. He created us. We are a child of the Almighty God. Why then should we ever be afraid or discouraged? Think up. Look up to heaven and ask our Heavenly Father for help, and then thank Him. Earthly fathers may fail us, but God, our Heavenly Father and Creator, will not.

Prayer: Thank You, God, for loving me, for giving me life, for caring for me. Thank You for sending Jesus into the world to take away my sins. You gave yourself as a sacrifice in my place because You loved me. Thank You is not enough. Amen.

Prayers, Thoughts, Gifts of Joy Today:

"Let the words of my mouth, and the meditation of my heart, be acceptable in thy sight, O Lord, my strength and my redeemer."

-PSALM 19:14

I try to pray this verse every morning before I get out of bed. The Lord is our strength, and He will help us keep our words acceptable to Him. When I have this verse, this prayer, this meditation in my heart, it makes my day go better in every way. What we say, what we think, what we dwell on will be better, and we will be happier because of this verse in our mind and heart. Speak words of kindness and encouragement. Meditate on good things. We can be strong because of God in our life today.

Prayer: "Let the words of my mouth, and the meditation of my heart, be acceptable in Thy sight, O Lord, my strength and my redeemer." Thank You. Amen.

Prayers, Thoughts, Gifts of Joy Today:

FEBRUARY 19

". . . see if I will not open you the windows of heaven, and pour you out a blessing, that there shall not be room enough to receive it."

-MALACHI 3:10

The Lord wants to bless us. He wants what is best for us, just as a loving, good parent wants the best for their children. The above verse is speaking of bringing your tithes and offerings to the Lord. When we read God's Word and follow His instructions, our life will go so much better. When we go our own stubborn way, our blessings and best are often quenched. We make the choice to follow God or go our own way, leaving Him behind. When we do this, His blessings and good are lost from us. Choose God and follow His way today, and watch His blessings flow to us.

Prayer: God, help me to follow You, to do Your will, to choose wisely. I ask for Your blessings on my life today. Thank You. Amen.

Prayers, Thoughts, Gifts of Joy Today:

> "... if God be for us, who can be against us? He that spared not his own Son, but delivered him up for us all, how shall he not with him also freely give us all things?"
>
> -ROMANS 8:32-33

God is for us! He is on our side, and He is ultimately the one in control. Nothing and no one can conquer us when we are sheltered in His care. He will save and deliver us. The Bible tells us so—believe it! When we are in doubt, have problems and troubles, heartaches and fears, we need to reread this powerful verse to help us stand strong. "If God be for us, who can be against us?" Who dare oppose God's child? He will help us through and give us the strength to keep on keeping on. It may sometimes seem in this world that the bad is winning, but it is not!!! God is in control! Remember this.

Prayer: God, You are my strength in times of trouble and in times of good. Protect me. Deliver me. Help me I pray today-this day-to make it through by Your power. Thank You. Amen.

Prayers, Thoughts, Gifts of Joy Today:

February 21

"My presence shall go with thee, and I will give thee rest."

-EXODUS 33:14

We can rest in God's love and presence. He promises to go with us. We can depend on Him in all things. All of us need to know that God goes with us. We can rest and relax in this fact. Quit trying to do it all, to fix everything for everybody. Breathe, rest, relax, step back, and just let God be God in our life. Give our troubles, problems, all we think we have to do to Him. He is there. He can help us through this. He will take care of us.

Prayer: Lord, go with me through this day and the week ahead. Help me with all I need to do, and give me Your rest and strength. Let me not grow weary, but have peace, calm, just breathe, and rely on You-not myself. You are in charge of this, not me. Thank You. Amen.

Prayers, Thoughts, Gifts of Joy Today:

"Blessed is the man that trusteth in the Lord, and whose hope the Lord is. For he shall be as a tree planted by the waters, and that spreadeth out her roots by the river, and shall not see when heat cometh, but her leaf shall be green, and shall not be careful in the year of drought, neither shall cease from yielding fruit."

-JEREMIAH 17:7-8

We are blessed because we trust in God. Let our faith grow deeper and stronger, and when problems come, let us remain hopeful, strong, and resilient because we are grounded and rooted in You. The winds, rain, storms, droughts, and diseases of life have no power over us when You are near, and we have put our faith and hope in You. The winds may blow and everything around us may be shaken and falling apart, but we can hold on to Your promises.

Prayer: Christ, be my rock, my firm and solid foundation on which I stand. When I am shaken and weathering the storms of life, hold my hand. Keep me in Your care. Thank You. Amen.

Prayers, Thoughts, Gifts of Joy Today:

". . . forgetting those things which are behind, and reaching forth unto those things which are before."

-PHILIPPIANS 3:13

Sometimes we have trouble moving on to new things, letting go of the past. There are some things we, of course, should remember—those who have gone before us, leaving us good memories and good values. Those who taught us well, those who loved and cared for us, we should remember. This verse is talking about letting go of the past that may hold us back from serving Jesus Christ, letting go of things that hold us back from fulfilling the full life Jesus has for us. Change is often difficult. One door closes, but it is hard to open and walk into a new way that is unfamiliar. Nostalgia, and living our life dreaming of the good old days may keep us from having the good new days God has planned for us. Be brave. Go!

Prayer: Help me to go and do what You have planned for me, Lord. Don't let me be afraid, but just let go and fly! Thank You. Amen.

Prayers, Thoughts, Gifts of Joy Today:

FEBRUARY 24

"Thou art my hiding place and my shield: I hope in thy word."

-PSALM 119:114

Hiding place: a safe place away from the things that can harm me. That is what I consider a hiding place to be. The Lord can be this for us—a hiding place and a shield from the problems and heartaches of life. We can have hope and security in His love and care. We know nothing can truly harm us when we are in His safety with His shield over us. We can rest securely in Him. When we are besieged by the troubles of this world, this verse gives us hope and rest. God is there for us to run to. He will embrace us in His arms and hide and shield us. He will give us hope.

Prayer: God, take me in Your arms of love, hide me, and shield me from evil. Renew my hope. Keep me safe until the storm passes by. Thank You. Amen.

Prayers, Thoughts, Gifts of Joy Today:

FEBRUARY 25

"He will fill thy mouth with laughing, and thy lips with rejoicing."

-**JOB 8:21**

The Bible talks a lot about rejoicing, joy, laughter, singing, dancing, and having a merry heart. This says to me that God wants us to be happy and filled with joy. Situations come into our lives that may make us sad, brokenhearted, unhealthy, or depressed, but God doesn't want this for His children. He wants to fill our mouths with laughter and our lips with praise again. We can rejoice and be glad, even when things aren't "perfect" because God is our strength and our song.

Prayer: Lord, let me laugh and rejoice again. Let my mouth praise You in all things. Give me a merry heart. Thank You. Amen.

Prayers, Thoughts, Gifts of Joy Today:

FEBRUARY 26

"I am the vine, ye are the branches: he that abideth in me, and I in him, the same bringeth forth much fruit: for without me ye can do nothing."
-John 15:5

Without God, we can do nothing; but with Him, we can do anything! He is our help, our power, our strength and is always there for us when we call out to Him. We should trust and depend on Him. Why should we worry or fear anyone or anything? God Almighty is on our side. If we abide in Him, He will allow us to bear fruit. Some of the fruits of the Spirit the Bible describes as "love, joy, peace, patience, kindness, goodness, faithfulness, gentleness, and self-control." Galatians 5:22-23. Strive for these fruits in life.

Prayer: God, help me to abide in You and Your Word and depend on You to do all things because without You, I can do nothing. Let me bear the fruits of Your Spirit. Thank You. Amen.

Prayers, Thoughts, Gifts of Joy Today:

"For he is our peace."

-EPHESIANS 2:14

He will give us peace. He is peace. He is not turmoil and disruption, but peace. Know this. Relax in this. When all around us gives way, when our life seems to be falling apart, He can be our hope and our peace. Don't worry and fret, but have trust and faith in the God of peace today, "For He is our peace."

Prayer: Help me today, Lord, and in the week ahead to trust You and You alone, not myself, not others, but You. Give me Your peace in my stressed and worried mind and heart. Calm me. Thank You. Amen.

Prayers, Thoughts, Gifts of Joy Today:

"Fear thou not; for I am with thee: be not dismayed; for I am thy God: I will strengthen thee; yea, I will help thee; yea, I will uphold thee with the right hand of righteousness."

-ISAIAH 41:10

Remember who is ultimately really in charge and stop worrying, okay? God is holding our hand through this life. Things may go wrong or not the way we want them, but He is our God and He sees the big picture. He loves us and wants the best for us. Our choices and decisions are sometimes wrong and cause us grief and worry. We can always ask forgiveness and ask God to help us through. When problems not of our own making, but due to life situations, come into our lives, He is there to strengthen us, hold our hand, and help.

Prayer: Thank You, Lord, for holding my hand today and not letting me go. I won't be afraid or anxious because I have You as my God. I will remember who is in charge and stop worrying. Help me through this day. Thank You. Amen.

Prayers, Thoughts, Gifts of Joy Today:

"Blessed be God, even the Father of our Lord Jesus Christ, the Father of mercies, and the God of all comfort. Who comforteth us in all our tribulations, that we may be able to comfort them which are in any trouble, by the comfort we ourselves are comforted of God."

-2 CORINTHIANS 1:3-4

When we go through a problem, a hurt, a heartbreak, God will comfort us if we ask. The Bible tells us He is a God of mercy and comfort. After going through these things, we are more able then to help others who are going through similar struggles and hurts. Often our problems and struggles will make us into stronger, more compassionate people. Watch for those in our life who need our comfort and reach out to them. Help others as God has helped us.

Prayer: God of mercy and comfort, thank You for helping me through. Help me to help comfort and show Your love to others who are struggling and hurting today. Thank You. Amen.

Prayers, Thoughts, Gifts of Joy Today:

MARCH 1

"He is not here: for he is risen, as he said."
-MATTHEW 28:6

Christ the Lord is risen. We serve a risen Savior! Hallelujah! Christians should be the most joyful people on the earth. Why are we often down and discouraged? Because we allow the world to steal our joy. We let ourselves forget we serve a risen Savior, an all-powerful God. Today, think on this fact. Think about the upcoming Easter event and why we celebrate the resurrection. Be happy, rejoice, sing, praise God for we, of all people, are most blessed.

Prayer: Praise to You God for all Your blessings that flow into my life. Thank You, Lord, for spring, for Your love, Your new life for us. Let me think on the meaning of Easter and praise You for all You did and keep on doing for me. Thank You. Amen.

Prayers, Thoughts, Gifts of Joy Today:

March 2

". . . I am with you always, even unto the end of the world."

-Matthew 28:20

Think on this. God is with us always, even until the end of this world. This verse and promise should give us great comfort and joy. He is there with us through all things. All we go through, He, our Lord, is there with us. Sometimes it feels as though we are all alone, doesn't it? But we are never alone. God is with us. After my husband died, one night I was in bed watching TV and all the lights went out. The electricity was out, and all was pitch black and quiet. For a moment, I felt a bit scared and all alone, but I began to pray and immediately realized I was not alone. I felt a calm and a peace that God gave me.

Prayer: Thank You, Lord, that You never leave me alone to face fears, problems, worries, and life. You say You will be with me always, and I believe this. Thank You. Amen.

Prayers, Thoughts, Gifts of Joy Today:

MARCH 3

"Wait on the Lord: be of good courage, and he shall strengthen thine heart: wait, I say, on the Lord."

-**PSALM 27:14**

We should have courage because the Bible tells us our Lord will give us strength. Remember: "With God we can do all things." Waiting is the hard part for me; waiting on God. His time and our time are very different. I want things to happen quickly. I am always in a hurry. But God is not in a hurry. He is teaching me how to wait in my life, to not get so flustered, anxious, and upset over things. He is in control—not me. What do we need to wait on today? Pray and remain calm. God is in control. He will give us the strength we need.

Prayer: Lord, give me strength, courage, and Your wisdom to wait, listen, and watch for Your guidance in my life today. Thank You. Amen.

Prayers, Thoughts, Gifts of Joy Today:

"The Lord is my light and my salvation; whom shall I fear? The Lord is the strength of my life; of whom shall I be afraid?"

-PSALM 27:1

When I am lonely and afraid, I repeat this verse aloud. It helps me. Try it. Why should we, as Christians, allow Satan to scare us into fear? The Almighty God gives us strength, courage, and light to overcome fear. God is light; in Him there is no darkness. Let us remember this. When we are discouraged, let us look to the light. Think up!

Prayer: God of light and my salvation, keep me strong and brave. Let me trust in You and not be afraid. You are my strength, my joy, my song, and my light. Thank You. Amen.

Prayers, Thoughts, Gifts of Joy Today:

MARCH 5

"God is our refuge and strength, a very present help in trouble. Therefore, we will not fear . . . . The Lord of hosts is with us; the God of Jacob is our refuge. . . . Be still, and know that I am God."

-PSALM 46:1, 2, 7, & 10

Stop striving, fretting, and running in all directions with our mind and body. "Be still" and know that God is there! We can relax, breathe, and be still in this knowledge. He is our hiding place, our strength, our comfort, and help. We don't have to do it all alone. The Lord is there for us and with us. When we find ourselves getting caught up in the hectic frenzy of life, we should stop, breathe, and receive His calm assurance. He is there with us through it all.

Prayer: Oh God, my Savior, my comforter and help, keep me in Your calming arms today. Bring to my mind peace and calm. Thank You. Amen.

Prayers, Thoughts, Gifts of Joy Today:

"But my God shall supply all your needs according to his riches in glory by Christ Jesus."
-PHILIPPIANS 4:19

G od will supply all our needs. Our needs and wants are different, of course. When we pray and lean on God, He will meet all our needs. We lack nothing when He is our Lord. Ask God to allow us to really see the difference between our real needs and things that do not matter in the grand scheme of things. What truly matters to us? Think on these. Put our heart and time into these. We will see that these turn out to be people rather than things. Those we love matter. Goodness matters. How we treat people matters.

Prayer: Oh God, let me trust in You to supply my needs and stop worrying about things of no consequence. Give me wisdom to discern my needs from my wants. Thank You. Amen.

Prayers, Thoughts, Gifts of Joy Today:

"For as the earth bringeth forth her bud, and as the garden causeth the things that are sown in it to spring forth; so the Lord God will cause righteousness and praise to spring forth."

-ISAIAH 61:11

Spring is a glorious season when fresh green grass, buds, and leaves begin to come out of the earth. This is a time of renewal and great joy. The earth seems to be singing joyously. Our Lord made the earth and caused these miracles to happen. Spring is a time of new life and rejoicing, a time of renewal. Praise His name and His wondrous works.

"After winter always comes spring."

-UNKNOWN AUTHOR

Prayer: Lord, my voice praises You today for all Your mighty works, the wonder and majesty of spring. Thank You for spring green, flowers, and birdsong. Amen.

Prayers, Thoughts, Gifts of Joy Today:

MARCH 8

"I have set the Lord always before me: because he is at my right hand, I shall not be moved. Therefore my heart is glad, and my glory rejoiceth: my flesh also shall rest in hope."

-PSALM 16:8-9

I will not be moved. We should repeat this aloud. Some translations give this word moved as shaken, and I like that. I will not be shaken. Because the Lord is always with me and holds my hand, I feel secure in His help and protection. My heart is glad. I rejoice, and I have peace and rest. And I have hope because of my God! Hope is a wonderful blessing from God. We, as Christians, have a blessed hope. Our hope is built on Jesus Christ. He is our hope and our stay. We will not be moved or shaken. We have a firm foundation in Jesus Christ.

Prayer: Thank You, Lord, that You are my hope and stay. Hold my right hand and keep always before me, guiding me through. Keep me strong. Thank You. Amen.

Prayers, Thoughts, Gifts of Joy Today:

MARCH 9

"Come unto me, all ye that labor and are heavy laden; and I will give you rest."

-MATTHEW 11:28

Are we sometimes weary and tired? Of course we are. God will give us rest and peace. Turn to Him. Give our burden, our struggles to the Lord. He can handle these for us. He will help us through our difficulties. Sometimes I feel overwhelmed with life and beaten down. It seems sometimes that wrong is winning, but God is still in control! When we feel ourselves falling or struggling, turn to God, pray, and call on Him. He will be there for us always. His Word promises this to us. Take courage and strength from His Word. He will never leave us or forsake us.

Prayer: Oh Lord, help me today, I pray. I am weary and burdened. Lift me up. Hold me up and let me stand on Your promises. Thank You. Amen.

Prayers, Thoughts, Gifts of Joy Today:

"We are troubled on every side, yet not distressed; we are perplexed, but not in despair; persecuted, but not forsaken; cast down, but not destroyed."

-2 CORINTHIANS 4:8-9

We may have troubles, but we have God on our side. Never give up or give in to defeat, because we are a child of the King of Kings! He is there to lift us up. We will not be distressed, in despair, forsaken, or destroyed because He is with us. God will allow us, as His children, to go through troubles and trials, but He will not allow us to be destroyed. He will save us and bring us out on the other side. Read the story of Job and Noah in the Bible. These will give us hope to grow closer to God while going through our troubles. Pray. Read the Bible and turn to Him for help.

Prayer: Lord Jesus, help me through my struggle. Draw me closer to You. Hold my hand. Lift me up. Help me to make it through today. Thank You. Amen.

Prayers, Thoughts, Gifts of Joy Today:

"Let your conversation be without covetous-ness; and be content with such things as ye have: for he hath said, I will never leave thee, nor forsake thee. So that we may boldly say, The Lord is my helper, and I will not fear what man shall do unto me."

-HEBREWS 13:5-6

Contentment with what we have is a hard thing. We seem to be bombarded by things, the desire for more things, with the advertisement world enticing us everywhere we turn. God reminds us in these verses to refrain from coveting (always wanting more or wanting what others have). Some translations say, "Let your character be free from the love of money. . . ." God does not say not to want nice things, or not to work for nice things, but He warns against the love and desires that are out of control, where things rule us and we aren't content and happy. God is with us and will help us in this.

Prayer: Lord, help me to have a contented and thankful spirit. Thank You. Amen.

Prayers, Thoughts, Gifts of Joy Today:

". . . they that wait upon the Lord shall renew their strength; they shall mount up with wings as eagles; they shall run and not be weary; and they shall walk and not faint."

-ISAIAH 40:31

Waiting is a hard thing for me. How about you? Praying to the Lord about a problem and then waiting for His answer takes lots of prayer. God says He will renew our strength and help us, lift us up as on eagles' wings, and we can run the race of life and not grow weary or faint beneath the struggles. Let the Lord help us today. Take this verse to heart. Reread it. Memorize it, and then apply it to your life. When we allow God to help us, He will.

Prayer: Oh God, renew my strength. Help me to run, walk, and fly spiritually. My soul will be set free in Your love. Help me to wait on You and not run ahead alone. Thank You. Amen.

Prayers, Thoughts, Gifts of Joy Today:

"The angel of the Lord encampeth round about them that fear him, and delivereth them."

-PSALM 34:7

God sends His angels to surround us and take care of us. When we fear the Lord, this means we revere Him, honor Him, and try to live to please Him. It doesn't mean we are frightened by our Heavenly Father, but know that He is all-powerful, holy, and just, and because of this, we have a respect for who He truly is. We are His child and He loves us, and just as an earthly parent will discipline and correct their child for the child's own good, even more does our Heavenly Father know what is for our best good. This verse promises us His care and deliverance.

Prayer: Thank You, Heavenly Father, for sending Your angels to surround me today and to watch over me. This gives me great assurance. Thank You. Amen.

Prayers, Thoughts, Gifts of Joy Today:

". . . therefore have I hope."

-LAMENTATIONS 3:21

I have hope! We, as Christians, have a great hope because of our Lord Jesus Christ and His salvation. He has mercy and forgiveness for us. We can hope in Him. He promises over and over throughout His Word to be with us, to love us, to protect us, to bring us through our trials, to hold our hand, to carry us, and to lift us up. Read His Word and be refreshed and uplifted. Above all, He promises us heaven and eternal life with Him. Hallelujah. Amen.

Prayer: Thank You, God, for hope-hope in all circumstances, the hope of tomorrow, and Your wonderful promises. I stand on Your promises! Thank You. Amen.

Prayers, Thoughts, Gifts of Joy Today:

MARCH 15

> "... blessed are ye that weep now; for ye shall laugh."
>
> -LUKE 6:21

Laughter—God's great gift to us! How blessed are we when we can laugh again or feel joy again after we have come through a crisis in our lives where we have wept and grieved. Laughter is a cleansing, a triumph to our soul. We may go through sorrows, troubles, and pains, but God is there for us to help carry us through. He will put laughter in our mouths once again and joy into our hearts. He is a God who cares deeply when we weep.

Prayer: Thank You, God, for the gift of laughter in my life. Help me to laugh again, to feel joy again. Thank You for delivering me from the dark tunnel of grief. Thank You. Amen.

Prayers, Thoughts, Gifts of Joy Today:

MARCH 16

"Be anxious for nothing, but in everything by prayer and supplication with thanksgiving let your requests be made known to God."

-PHILIPPIANS 4:6

Don't worry about anything. Wow! That is a mouthful, isn't it? Why do we worry? Because we don't fully trust God? That is the bottom line. We aren't certain He will take care of us the way we want. We tell ourselves He loves us and wants the best for us, but we see pain and suffering around us and are afraid that we may have to suffer or endure pain, and we do not want this. We want a life free from pain and sorrows, right? Somewhere deep down we know that this life on earth does carry pain and sorrow; it's not heaven yet. We can only trust God with everything and trust Him to carry us through.

Prayer: Lord, help me not to worry and fret so much. It is all in Your hands, not mine. I give my illusion of control of my life over to You. Guide me. Lead me. Give me Your wisdom. Thank You. Amen.

Prayers, Thoughts, Gifts of Joy Today:

"Whoso putteth his trust in the Lord shall be safe."

-PROVERBS 29:25

Trust in the Lord, and He will keep us safe. When I am afraid, I have learned to pray aloud to the Lord, and immediately, I feel a sense of peace and calm. I have learned to depend on Him more and more because He is my strength and my shield. When we feel alone, scared, worried, or upset, pray to Him. He will listen to those who call out to Him and help us. This doesn't mean that everything in our life will become perfect, but it means He will give us the strength and power to get through it, change it, or deal with it, whatever the "it" is. We can depend on our Lord!

Prayer: Lord, I call out to You today for help with _____. Show me how to deal with this. Help me. Thank You. Amen.

Prayers, Thoughts, Gifts of Joy Today:

MARCH 18

"Ointment and perfume rejoice the heart: so doth the sweetness of a man's friend by hearty counsel."

-**PROVERBS 27:9**

Sweet smells and oils bring joy to our lives. I personally love the scents of some candles and use lavender oil in a diffuser beside my bed at night to help me sleep. There are scents that soothe and comfort us. This verse compares this to the sweetness of a dear friend who stands beside us and helps comfort and soothe us. God is good to give us friends. If you have a good friend, treasure their friendship. To have a friend, we also have to be a friend. Think of others. Be there for them. It's not all about us and what friends can do for us, but also about what we can do to minister to and help them. We should get outside of ourselves and our own wants and be thankful always for our friends, who are like an ointment of healing and a perfume of great worth to us.

Prayer: Thank You, Lord, for my friends. I am blessed by them. Help me to be a true friend and blessing to them today. Thank You. Amen.

Prayers, Thoughts, Gifts of Joy Today:

"Thou, even thou, art Lord alone; thou hast made heaven, the heaven of heavens, with all their host, the earth, and all things that are therein, the seas, and all that is therein, and thou preservest them all; and the host of heaven worshippeth thee."

-NEHEMIAH 9:6

Awe, the majesty of our Lord God Almighty! He alone is the Lord. "It is He who hath made us and not we ourselves." (Psalm 100:3) Since He made the heavens, the earth, the seas, and all that is within them—including we humans—how can we doubt Him? We should not doubt Him! We should bow down in awe and worship before Him and give our lives to Him each new morning of our life. Praise and honor are due Him.

Prayer: Oh Lord, today I stand in awe of You when I read this verse and really think on what You have done. It is beyond the grasp of my mind, but my heart feels it. Thank You is not enough! Amen.

Prayers, Thoughts, Gifts of Joy Today:

"Even the hairs on your head are all numbered. Fear not therefore: ye are of more value than many sparrows."

-LUKE 12:7

The verses prior to this speak about God not forgetting even the little sparrows and how much more He does care for us. He has made us and knows everything about us—even how many hairs are on our head. We have an all-powerful God, a creator, a protector, a lover of our souls. He cares. We can cast all our cares on Him today. Look to God, not circumstances. Circumstances change; God does not. Let go of problems and trust them to God who knows us, really knows us, made us, and to whom we are of great value.

Prayer: Lord, today I put my problems into Your capable hands. I cannot handle this alone or without You. Help me, I pray. Help me to not fear and to not worry, but to trust You to take this burden. Thank You. Amen.

Prayers, Thoughts, Gifts of Joy Today:

MARCH 21

"Which of you with taking thought can add to his stature one cubit? If ye then be not able to do that thing which is least, why take ye thought for the rest? Consider the lilies how they grow: they toil not, they spin not; and yet I say unto you, that Solomon in all his glory was not arrayed like one of these. If then God so clothe the grass, which is today in the field, and tomorrow is cast into the oven; how much more will he clothe you, O ye of little faith?"

-LUKE 12:25-28

We can change not one single thing by worrying over it, so why are we worrying? God cares for us and He knows our problems, our pains, and our situation. Our Heavenly Father, who made us, loves and cares about us. We are repeatedly told this in the scriptures, so believe it! Accept it. Live it. Live in a state of rest, knowing God is ultimately in charge and will lead us to a solution.

Prayer: God, thank You for taking my burdens, my worries, and cares. I will trust You today to help me through, direct, and guide me. Give me Your wisdom. Thank You. Amen.

Prayers, Thoughts, Gifts of Joy Today:

"The Lord is thy keeper; the Lord is thy shade upon thy right hand. The sun shall not smite thee by day, nor the moon by night. The Lord shall preserve thee from all evil; he shall preserve thy soul. The Lord shall preserve thy going out and thy coming in from this time forth, and even for evermore."

-PSALM 121:5-8

The Lord will take care of us, His children. He watches over us and is the keeper of our soul. On this earth, we cannot fathom the true meaning of eternity. It is beyond us. God has a heaven and an eternity planned for us. We can rest knowing this. We spend so much time planning for today and tomorrow, but do we plan for our eternity? This is what really matters. Where we will spend eternity matters. Think on this today.

Prayer: O God, help me to have even more faith and trust in You today. I trust You with everything in my life today, knowing that You and You alone are my source of strength and calm. When the world around me spirals out of my control, it is still in Your control. Thank You. Amen.

Prayers, Thoughts, Gifts of Joy Today:

"For we walk by faith, not by sight. We are confident, I say, and willing rather to be absent
from the body, and to be present with the Lord.
Wherefore we labour, that, whether present or
absent, we may be acceptable of him."

-2 CORINTHIANS 5:7-9

It should be our ambition, as God's children, to be pleasing
and acceptable to Him. We are to walk by faith and not
by sight. We should not allow the problems of the world to
get us down and discourage us because if we have faith and
believe God's Word, we know the final victory belongs to the
Lord our God. Faith in God strengthens us daily to go forward, to conquer things in our life that bind us.

Prayer: God, help me to have even more faith and trust
in You today. I trust You with everything in my life today,
knowing that You and You alone are my source of strength
and calm when the world around me spirals out of control.
Thank You. Amen.

Prayers, Thoughts, Gifts of Joy Today:

"Every good gift and every perfect gift is from above, and cometh down from the Father of lights, with whom is no variableness, neither shadow of turning."

-JAMES 1:17

God is the Father of light. There is no darkness in Him. He is the same always, and we can put our trust in Him. Trusting and letting go is hard for us sometimes. Our God is faithful to us and proves to us over and over that we can trust Him. He gives to us good and perfect gifts always.

We should thank Him daily for His good and perfect gifts.

Prayer: Lord, thank You for every good gift You have given me. Thank You that You do not change, but stay constant and reliable, firm and true. In this unsteady world, You are my rock. Thank You. Amen.

Prayers, Thoughts, Gifts of Joy Today:

MARCH 25

**"The earth is the Lord's, and the fullness thereof;
the world, and they that dwell therein."**

-PSALM 24:1

Spring is a wonderful time to enjoy the world the Lord has made. We see the fullness of the earth budding and blooming, opening up to heaven, and we stand in awe of the earth's beauty. Flowers blooming in all their glorious colors, and their sweet fragrance drifting up to heaven, is a taste of heaven on earth. Our loving God created this beauty for us to enjoy. It is amazing and wondrous when we really think that God gave us this gift to enjoy!

Prayer: God, creator of heaven and earth and all their wonders and beauty, I stand amazed and so thankful today. When I look at a beautiful flower and smell its fragrance, I think of You and marvel at the fact that You created this beauty for me to enjoy. Thank You. Amen.

Prayers, Thoughts, Gifts of Joy Today:

"For with God nothing shall be impossible."
-LUKE 1:37

Nothing shall be impossible for us if God is with us! Do we believe this? Yes, but do we live as if we believe this? Probably not. We trust God, but not ourselves, and we second-guess and question our decisions, our motives, and plans. We hold ourselves back because of our self-doubt. Oh what we could accomplish if we would really trust God! Anything is possible with God on our side. So go for it today! Pray. Ask. Believe. Step out in faith. Ready-Set-Go for it! Nothing is impossible for God!

Prayer: Lord, I know this is true and still sometimes I doubt. Help me to really accept this and live this way, knowing that all things are possible with You by my side today. Thank You. Amen.

Prayers, Thoughts, Gifts of Joy Today:

MARCH 27

"My grace is sufficient for thee: for my strength is made perfect in weakness. Most gladly therefore will I rather glory in my infirmities, that the power of Christ may rest upon me."

-2 CORINTHIANS 12:9

Grace and God's strength can be in our life today. Oh, how wonderful! His grace is enough to get us through whatever challenge we face. We are weak, but He is strong. Our weakness, our frailty, our shortcomings He can take and turn into strengths through His grace. He can make us strong, and He can cause us to be used by Him and turn bad into good, for His glory.

Prayer: Lord, when I am weak, You make me strong when I trust in You. I realize just how lost, weak, and helpless I am without You in my life. Give me Your strength today in all I do. Thank You. Amen.

Prayers, Thoughts, Gifts of Joy Today:

"Submit yourselves therefore to God. Resist the devil, and he will flee from you. Draw nigh to God, and he will draw nigh to you."

-JAMES 4:7-8

Think on God and His ways, resist and turn away from evil thoughts and actions. It is hard some days to resist things the devil tempts us with. But if we stay near God, pray, and read His Word, it gets easier to keep ourselves from wrong choices. I pray each day for God to help me to choose wisely and stay in His will because I know without His guidance, my life would be a mess. Wrong choices bring about devastating consequences. We can trust God to help us when we ask for His help. He wants to give us the best. He doesn't want us to choose badly and go the wrong way. He will help us when we want to live our lives in His will.

Prayer: Dear Lord, today help me to live near to You and resist the devil and any form of evil or wrong. It is so easy to fall into envy, hate, and other wrong actions. When I am near You, these things slip away. Keep my mind on You. Thank You. Amen.

Prayers, Thoughts, Gifts of Joy Today:

MARCH 29

"Make a joyful noise unto the Lord, all ye lands. Serve the Lord with gladness: come before his presence with singing. Know ye that the Lord he is God: it is he that hath made us, and not we ourselves; we are his people, and the sheep of his pasture."

-PSALM 100:1-3

Sing to the Lord. Praise Him. Serve Him with gladness, happiness, and joy! He is our God, our Savior. He made us, created us, and we are His people. He loves us and cares about our lives and our happiness, because we are His children. Just as a shepherd watches over his sheep and wants to keep them safe and secure, so does God care for us, our needs, and our condition.

He cares and loves us and wants only good—not evil—for us. He has our best in mind always.

Prayer: Thank You, God, for watching over me. Thank You for Your love and care. Let me sing and praise Your name forever, for You have done great things for me. I worship You today. Thank You. Amen.

Prayers, Thoughts, Gifts of Joy Today:

> "Two are better than one; because they have a
> good reward for their labor. For if they fall, the
> one will lift up his fellow: but woe to him that
> is alone when he falleth; for he hath not another
> to help him up."
>
> -ECCLESIASTES 4:9-10

We need to be there for each other and to lift others up when they fall or stumble. When we work together for the same goal, it doubles our capacity to get things done. Think of others. Help others to succeed, to achieve, to accomplish their goals and dreams. We don't have to go alone through struggles or work. There are others there to help us. When I go through a problem or heartache, hurt or struggle, friends and loved ones are there to help me. I appreciate their help, and then I try to be there for them when they need me. The Lord gives us friends, family, others in our lives to help us get through it more easily. Don't be afraid to ask for help when you need it. This does not show weakness, but really shows you are strong and secure enough to ask for help.

Prayer: Lord, thank You for loved ones and friends who are there for me when I fall down. You send them to lift me up again. Let me be there to lift them as well. Thank You. Amen.

Prayers, Thoughts, Gifts of Joy Today:

"I love them that love me; and those that seek me early shall find me."

-Proverbs 8:17

S eek the Lord early in the morning, when we first wake. Begin each day with Him, and ask for His presence all the day through. Our day, our life will be happier and blessed when we do this. The Lord loves us and wants the best for us. Open up to His blessings and love daily. Early seek Him. He says He loves us. Accept this. Be joyful in this fact. Can we believe that God loves us? He does; He really does. The Bible tells us so.

Prayer: Oh God, thank You for Your love and care, and for watching over me and my life. I come to You early this morning seeking Your face and asking for Your protection over me today. Keep me in Your arms. Thank You. Amen.

Prayers, Thoughts, Gifts of Joy Today:

APRIL 1

"If we confess our sins, he is faithful and just to forgive us our sins, and to cleanse us from all unrighteousness."

-1 JOHN 1:9

Confess our sins and God will forgive us? Amazing, isn't it? Simple, yet true. To worship a God who forgives us when we come to Him and say "I am sorry" is a blessing that will bring us great peace in our heart. Walking around with guilt on our heart and mind will bog us down, causing us pain. He wants to lift these sin burdens off our hearts if we go to Him in prayer and repentance and just ask Him to forgive us. It's that simple. It is called mercy and grace.

Prayer: Thank You, Lord Jesus, that You forgive me when I confess and ask You to forgive me. It is enough. Thank You. Amen.

Prayers, Thoughts, Gifts of Joy Today:

APRIL 2

"For ye shall go out with joy, and be led forth with peace: the mountains and the hills shall break forth before you into singing, and all the trees of the field shall clap their hands."

-ISAIAH **55:12**

This is a wonderful verse for spring. We are to go out with joy and find sweet peace. The world around us will open up and sing for joy and burst forth in clapping and praise! What a beautiful word picture of joy and great happiness. Open yourself up to the beauty and wonder of all the Lord has given you to enjoy. He has blessed us with such glorious beauty and will give us peace as well if we will open ourselves to it. Go this morning outside alone—preferably to a garden—and pray. Be thankful and aware.

Prayer: Dear Lord Jesus, I praise Your name for the beauty of nature, for springtime, for Your love, joy, and peace; sweet peace. Thank You. Amen.

Prayers, Thoughts, Gifts of Joy Today:

APRIL 3

**"The Lord will give strength unto his people,
the Lord will bless his people with peace."**
-PSALM 29:11

S trength and peace: what a wonderful promise to us these gifts are. We are safe and secure in God's hands. Oh, that is good. When we have such a God as we do, why do we worry and fret? Because we lack faith and trust, I think. Even though I think I have faith and trust, I still often find myself worrying and stressing about things and people in my life. I pray for God to help me to trust Him more and to bless me with His peace.

Prayer: Oh God, help me to have more strength and peace, to trust in You and know that You hold me in Your arms right now. Nothing can touch me unless You allow it, and if You allow it, You will carry me through. Thank You. Amen.

Prayers, Thoughts, Gifts of Joy Today:

". . . I know whom I have believed, and am persuaded that he is able to keep that which I have committed unto him against that day."

-2 TIMOTHY 1:12

I believe in Jesus Christ for my salvation and believe He will keep my soul through eternity. I put my faith, my hope in His hands. That is enough! He has saved my soul. I am blessed! To have faith in God and be confident that He is able to keep us throughout life is something that we can't exactly put our finger on as to describe how we believe and trust. However, faith is an unseen and unexplained thing that God gives us. God gives us faith and secures us through faith. We can know, in our hearts, this to be true.

Prayer: Thank You, God, for saving my soul and giving me the promise of eternity in heaven with You. Thank You for giving me faith. Amen.

Prayers, Thoughts, Gifts of Joy Today:

April 5

"Let not your heart be troubled: ye believe in God, believe also in me."

-JOHN 14:1

God doesn't want us to be troubled and worried. There are so many verses throughout the Bible that tell us not to worry or be anxious: verses that encourage us to trust, to believe, and to put our hope in Jesus. He wants us to pray and draw near to Him, placing our worries and fears into His capable hands. He can handle all our problems and give us the strength and power to come through them. He will give us peace, strength for the day, and hope and courage to face whatever tomorrow may bring. We just have to ask Him.

Prayer: Lord, I come to You today with trust and hope. I put myself in Your hands. Take away all fear and troubles from my mind. Fill it with You. Thank You, Lord. Amen.

Prayers, Thoughts, Gifts of Joy Today:

APRIL 6

"I will greatly rejoice in the Lord; my soul shall be joyful in my God."

-ISAIAH 61:10

Rejoice and be joyful because we serve a great God! He has saved us and set us free from sin and the punishment of sin. We are blessed beyond measure, so we have much for which to be grateful and joyful. Praise Him and thank Him in all we do today. Even when things are not perfect in our lives, we can rejoice in the Lord because He gives us hope. Our soul, our spirit, our inner being can be filled with joy—an inner joy that surpasses an earthly, surface joy. Earthly joy, in things and people, can be taken away from us, but God's joy cannot.

Prayer: Oh Lord, my God, the joy giver, I praise Your name and thank You for giving me joy and rejoicing in this life. You tell me to be happy, to sing, to clap my hands, and rejoice, so I will. Thank You for the gifts of laughter, for love, for joy, for music, and all the beauty of the world. Thank You especially when I find true spiritual joy by drawing closer to You. Amen.

Prayers, Thoughts, Gifts of Joy Today:

APRIL 7

". . . Jesus spoke again unto them saying, 'I am the light of the world: he that followeth me shall not walk in darkness, but shall have the light of life.' "

-JOHN 8:12

Light, not darkness. Good, not bad. Know the difference. Jesus wants us to walk in the light, in the good, to know good from evil. We should strive to have our eyes open and be able to discern between what's right and what's wrong. Jesus gave us His Holy Spirit to live in us when we accept Him as our Savior, and His Holy Spirit guides us—if we allow guidance—and helps us to distinguish light from darkness. Pray today for His guidance. Often, it is difficult to perceive right from wrong in this world. Situations get convoluted, and today's society wants to muddy the waters of right and wrong and confuse our sense of knowing the difference. As Christians, God's children, we can pray and ask God's leadership, study His Word. God never goes against His Word and the principles of His Word. When in doubt, pray and ask God's wisdom, and then study His Word.

Prayer: Lord Jesus, help me today to follow You into light and shun darkness. You are the light of the world. Help me to truly know right from wrong, light from darkness. Thank You. Amen.

Prayers, Thoughts, Gifts of Joy Today:

"Blessed are the people that know the joyful sound: they shall walk, O Lord, in the light of thy countenance. In thy name they rejoice all the day."

-PSALM 89:15-16

We, as God's people, know joy when we walk with the Lord in the light of His presence. Seek His face early every morning as we start our day, and our day and life will go along so much more smoothly and joyfully. Knowing God doesn't mean we will have no more problems. It means we will have an all-powerful God to walk with us through our problems—one who will give us strength, courage, and hope to go on through this life with rejoicing and hope. Some people may teach that when we have God, we never have problems, but this just isn't true. Christians suffer. The difference is that when we do suffer, we have an advocate in God to help us bear our suffering. We are never alone. This doesn't mean it doesn't hurt or that God will take the problems away as we would want them taken or resolved, but He will go through it with us.

Prayer: Dear Lord, thank You for always being with me and helping me this day and every day. I rejoice all the day because of You. When I forget You are here with me, I start to stress, worry, and fret; but then I think of You, and I am strong. Thank You. Amen.

Prayers, Thoughts, Gifts of Joy Today:

APRIL 9

"The Lord thy God in the midst of thee is mighty; he will save, he will rejoice over thee with joy; he will rest in His love, he will joy over thee with singing."

-ZEPHANIAH 3:17

Our Lord loves us and takes pleasure over us, just as we do our children. He saves and restores us, blesses us, and watches over us. I love the above verse that says, ". . . He will joy over thee with singing." God created music and singing. When I think of this, it blesses me. I love to sing and appreciate music, and to realize that our God created music and wants us to have music in our lives is a wonderful gift to mankind. Singing blesses our soul and it blesses God. This verse states that God is mighty. We sometimes forget just how powerful and mighty our God is. When we think on this, it should give us great encouragement to know that we serve a mighty God—one who is able to defend us, save us, restore us, and help us in our life.

Prayer: God, thank You for music and the ability to appreciate it. Thank You for joy, rejoicing, singing, and praise. Thank You for being in our midst. Thank You. Amen.

Prayers, Thoughts, Gifts of Joy Today:

"And whatsoever ye do, do it heartily, as to the Lord, and not unto men."

-COLOSSIANS 3:23

Whatever we do, we are to do it wholeheartedly; give our all and our best to the work, as if we were doing it for God, not ourselves and not others. In this way, we will do our best and be happy and blessed. We will also have less doubt about our work. When we do our best, then we can let go and give it all over to God. He can even take our failures and make them successful. Pray, do your best, and then give it to God.

Prayer: Thank You, Jesus, for giving me the ability and desire to do this work. Guide me, lead me, and help me, I pray. I give my talents, my time, my very life to You right now. Make of me what You will. Thank You. Amen.

Prayers, Thoughts, Gifts of Joy Today:

"He that trusteth in the Lord, mercy shall compass him about."

-PSALM 32:10

This is another promise from God: if we thank Him and trust Him, we shall be surrounded by His mercy (another translation says loving kindness). Mercy is not getting what we deserve, but rather, being given forgiveness and a reprieve. Because God loves us, He wants what's best for us and treats us with love and mercy. Sometimes we may not feel as if we have been given mercy; we may have to go through the consequences of our sins on earth. But if we confess our sins, are truly sorry for them, and turn to God, He will forgive us and give us mercy.

Prayer: Jesus, thank You for your mercy and loving kindness toward me. I do trust in You and put my faith and life in Your hands. Thank You. Amen.

Prayers, Thoughts, Gifts of Joy Today:

APRIL 12

"Take My yoke upon you, and learn of me; for I am meek and lowly in heart: and ye shall find rest unto your soul. For my yoke is easy, and my burden is light."

-Matthew 11:29-30

Finding rest for our soul in this hectic, stress-filled world seems difficult, doesn't it? Rush, rush, rush—hurry, hurry, hurry—seems to be what we get caught up in. Resting in God's Word, praying, and thinking on God can and will relax us and bring peace and calm into our soul. Learn of Him. Study His Word. Be still and get to know Him. Find His peace, His quietness, His gentleness, His calm Spirit. The world around us may not be easy or light, but His is. Learn to be in His world. We can learn to take ourselves out of our stress-filled world when we pray and read God's Word more and ask for His help in being more peace-filled and calm in spirit. He is there for us. He asks us to learn more about Him and find His rest.

Prayer: Oh God, give me Your peace and calm today; right now. I will breathe slowly and relax into Your love. Thank You. Amen.

Prayers, Thoughts, Gifts of Joy Today:

> "My voice shalt thou hear in the morning, O Lord; in the morning will I direct my prayer unto thee, and will look up."
>
> **-PSALM 5:3**

There is an old song that talks about meeting God early in the morning while the dew is still out. When we seek Him early in the morning, pray, and ask for His guidance through our day, we are able to face the day positively and with the awareness that we are never alone. We will gain more courage and confidence, knowing we have asked God for help, and He will help us. If we look up to God for our strength, He will give it and always be with us, even through the most difficult times. God will be with you through the struggles and the joys of life, the highs and lows.

Prayer: Lord, I come to You early today and seek You. Be with me through this day. Together, with You, I can do this. Thank You. Amen.

Prayers, Thoughts, Gifts of Joy Today:

APRIL 14

"Because thou hast been my help, therefore in the shadow of thy wings will I rejoice."
-PSALM 63:7

We can rejoice because God is our help—has been and will always be. We, as Christians, have so many reasons to rejoice and be glad. Why do we allow things to get us down? We are looking at the wrong things if we are down and discouraged. We should turn our eyes, our minds, back on Jesus and then we can rejoice because He has been our help and hope, and He continues to be. Look to Him for our help, our strength, our courage, and then get ready to rejoice!

Prayer: You, O Lord, are my help. Thank You. I lift my eyes, my heart, my hands to You, Lord. I will be glad and rejoice because of You. Thank You. Amen.

Prayers, Thoughts, Gifts of Joy Today:

"For the eyes of the Lord run to and fro throughout the whole earth, to shew himself strong in the behalf of them whose heart is perfect toward him."

-2 CHRONICLES 16:9

God watches over us. He gives us his strong support if we trust Him and give our hearts and lives to Him. The above verse uses the word "perfect," and we know that we are never perfect; however, when we give Jesus control over our heart, He makes it perfect. It is in giving over our desires, our lives, ourselves to Jesus that we have His strength and help in our lives. He will help us daily. Just ask for His help.

Prayer: Thank You, Lord, for watching over me and giving me Your strong support. Let my heart be ever completely Yours, and let me live today to be a blessing to You and others. Thank You. Amen.

Prayers, Thoughts, Gifts of Joy Today:

"And even to your old age I am he; and even to gray hairs will I carry you. I have made, and I will bear; even I will carry, and will deliver you."
-ISAIAH 46:4

God will carry us throughout our lives, even into old age. He will see us through life and will be there for us. This is such a powerful and wonderful promise. We should rejoice in this! As we grow older, life may break us down at times. Just know that God is there with us—even in the darkest hours—and will carry and deliver us. Take strength and courage from this fact.

Prayer: O Lord, my God, I take courage from Your promise that You will be with me, will carry and deliver me, even into my old age and gray hairs. Thank You for being with me today and always. Amen.

Prayers, Thoughts, Gifts of Joy Today:

April 17

"The Lord hears thee in the day of trouble; the name of the God of Jacob defend thee; send thee help . . . and strengthen thee. . . ."

-Psalm 20:1-2

When we are in trouble, we can call on the Lord, our God, to help, defend, and strengthen us. He is there all the time—even in our loneliest and darkest hours. In our days of troubles, problems, heartaches, and brokenness, He is there to bring us out on the other side. I read a quote by Ernest Hemingway that said, "The world breaks everyone, and afterwards, many are stronger at the broken places." I thought, *This is so true*. Life does sometimes break us, but God can mend the brokenness, heal the heart, and give it strength again. We can become even stronger after going through life's difficulties, and often we become a better person after the fires of troubles.

Prayer: Lord, heal me, strengthen me, and help me today. Fix the broken places and make them strong again. Mold me into the person You want me to become for You. Thank You. Amen.

Prayers, Thoughts, Gifts of Joy Today:

APRIL 18

"Now the Lord of peace Himself give you peace always by all means. The Lord be with you."
-2 THESSALONIANS 3:16

Peace, calm, gentleness; these I want in my life. How about you? The Lord Jesus Christ is the only one to give us true peace. Pray and ask Him today. His peace is a peace that surpasses all understanding. When all around you there may be turmoil and strife, He can give you a calmness that transcends understanding, a peace of the heart. Let nothing disturb you; He is in control. Let nothing shake you; He is in control. Give control of your life to Him and have peace. It is when we struggle against Him that we have the most turmoil. He tells us to be still and know that He is God. Being still in His presence will bring us peace.

Prayer: Lord of peace and comfort, give me Your peace and calm the storms of my life. Let me rest in Your love and gentle care. Thank You. Amen.

Prayers, Thoughts, Gifts of Joy Today:

APRIL 19

"Therefore . . . be ye steadfast, unmovable, always abounding in the work of the Lord, forasmuch as ye know, that your labor is not in vain in the Lord."

-1 CORINTHIANS 15:8

Stand firm, never give up, keep on keeping on, for the labor that you do for the Lord will not be in vain. Sometimes I get tired, and I know you do as well. We are human. We get discouraged and down. When this happens, read and reread verses of encouragement like the above verse to recharge and hang on. Our labor will not be in vain. The Lord will help us and lift us up. He will hold our hand through this life—even in the most difficult moments—and see us through to the end. His Word gives us this promise.

Prayer: Oh Lord, my God, keep me steadfast and steady. Hold my hand. Lift me up. Let me work on for You. Thank You. Amen.

Prayers, Thoughts, Gifts of Joy Today:

APRIL 20

"The Lord is my strength and my shield; my heart trusted in him, and I am helped; therefore my heart greatly rejoiceth; and with my song will I praise him."

-PSALM 28:7

He will be our strength and our shield; what a blessing. With the Lord beside us, we can remain strong and fearless. Put our trust in Him today. Lean on His unchanging arms. He will help us through it all, day by day. Then thank Him, praise Him, sing songs of praise to Him. The Bible tells us again and again that He loves praise and songs. The Lord God created music and song. Just thinking about God liking music makes me happy. He puts a song in our hearts, if we will just sing it for Him. How wonderful is this?

Prayer: O Lord, thank You for Your strength today, for helping me through. I rejoice and praise You and lift up my songs to You. Thank You for the gift of music and song. Amen.

Prayers, Thoughts, Gifts of Joy Today:

APRIL 21

"I will sing of thy power; yea, I will sing aloud of thy mercy in the morning; for thou hast been my defense and refuge in the day of my trouble. Unto thee, O my strength, will I sing: for God is my defense, and the God of my mercy."

-PSALM 59:16-17

Sing praises to the Lord for all His mercies, His help in times of trouble, and His unfailing love. Where would we be if not for God? I know I need Him every day in my life. He is my defender, my help in times of trouble. I run to Him for help and for shelter from a troubling world. Troubles, worries. Just the everyday little and big problems threaten to take away our serenity, our hope, our joy, but we can run to God and He holds us safely from the world. We can and do put our trust in Him. When we depend on God, and not ourselves, it takes much of the pressure of living off us. We can relax, knowing that God has us in His hand. We are secure and safe because of this. He is our defense and refuge in times of trouble. Praise Him today!

Prayer: I will sing to You this morning songs of praise, worship, and thanksgiving. Oh Lord, thank You for being my shield, my defense, my Savior. Amen.

Prayers, Thoughts, Gifts of Joy Today:

"For whatsoever is born of God overcometh the world: and this is the victory that overcometh the world, even our faith."

-1 JOHN 5:4

We need to remind ourselves who really is in charge and think "victory" because of our faith in God! He has already overcome the world and Satan. When we read the Bible, we are told how the story ends. We put our faith, our hope, and our trust in the Lord. Thank Him for this great promise—it can become our verse for life. He will help us to have even stronger faith.

Prayer: Thank You, God, for overcoming the world and evil. Help me today to overcome every doubt and fear, to trust You more and more. Why should I ever be afraid? You have won, and I am on Your side-the winning side. Thank You. Amen.

Prayers, Thoughts, Gifts of Joy Today:

APRIL 23

"Jesus said, 'With men this is impossible; but with God all things are possible.'"

-**MATTHEW 19:26**

Impossible. We use this word often, or at least we think it often. We feel overwhelmed, that it is impossible to go on in a situation. We feel fear, worry, stress, or become anxious. Jesus said, "With God all things are possible," so we can believe this to be absolutely true. Today, let's turn our concerns, our worries, this overwhelming situation over to God. With Him by our side, holding our hand, we can do the impossible! We can make it through this—whatever this is!

Prayer: Thank You, Lord, that ALL things are possible with You. With You by my side, holding my hand, I can know that it is possible! Take away my worry and doubt and replace them with strength and courage. I can make it through this (whatever this is)! Thank You. Amen.

Prayers, Thoughts, Gifts of Joy Today:

APRIL 24

"My soul, wait thou only upon God; for my expectation is from him."

My expectation, my hope is from God. Wait and rest; relax in Him. Don't always be in such a hurry. Learn to relax and trust God. Often, we are rushing around so frantically, going in so many different directions, that we miss God's still, small voice and guidance for today, right now, in this very moment of our life. "Be still," He says, "and know that I am God." Be still. Be quiet. Be calm. Relax. Breathe. Push away all stress, the loudness, and the busyness of the moment. Pray and wait; expect great things.

Prayer: God, I come to You in this quiet moment, peaceful, still, waiting, and listening. Still my soul. Calm my spirit. Give me Your sweet peace. My hope is in You. Thank You. Amen.

Prayers, Thoughts, Gifts of Joy Today:

APRIL 25

"The Lord also will be a refuge for the oppressed, a refuge in times of trouble. And they that know thy name will put their trust in thee: for thou, Lord, hast not forsaken them that seek thee."

-PSALM 9:9-10

When we are down and discouraged, thinking low thoughts, we can take refuge in the Lord. He will lift us up if we ask for His help. He has never forsaken us. He is always there for us when we reach out to Him and trust Him. In times of trouble, He will bring us through. Just think back on where you have been and all that He has brought you through already. Keep on trusting Him.

"I will not allow the negative things in my life to spoil all the good things I have. I choose to be happy."

-ZIG ZIGLAR

Prayer: O God, I trust in You! I know You have never forsaken me. You are my refuge and strength. Let me love and trust You more. Thank You. Amen.

Prayers, Thoughts, Gifts of Joy Today:

"Bear ye one another's burdens, and so fulfill the law of Christ."

-GALATIANS 6:2

B ear the burdens of others? I have a hard enough time handling my own, don't you? Christ said to do this, so I will try. We can pray for and with others, really show that we care, and in this way help to bear their burdens. I know personally that after my husband died, the letters and cards from others really helped me. It showed me others cared that I was hurting and cared that he was gone. A note, a hug, just to cry with someone can help. The main thing is to be aware that others have burdens, and then open your heart to try and help them. Get outside of yourself and do something for someone else today. Make this a goal in life—to help others.

Prayer: Lord, let me see others' burdens, be aware, and willing to help. Let me be a blessing to someone's life today for Your glory. Thank You. Amen.

Prayers, Thoughts, Gifts of Joy Today:

**"And when ye stand praying forgive, if ye have
ought against any; that our Father also which is
in heaven may forgive you your trespasses."**

-MARK 11:25

Forgiveness. This is a tough one, isn't it? Well, it is for me, anyway. When someone has hurt us, wronged us, and they don't ask for forgiveness, are we to forgive them anyway? Jesus Christ tells us to repent (be sorry for our sins) and ask Him for forgiveness before He forgives us. When we do this, He does forgive us. He doesn't forgive unless we ask for forgiveness. So I understand that when someone asks for our forgiveness, we should forgive. But what if they don't ask. What if they don't even seem to notice or care that we have been hurt? I believe we should pray and let the hurt—the wrong we feel has been done to us—go. If not, it will eat us up. We should pray for that person and for ourselves and forgive as best we can for our own sake. Pray and give them to God. He knows best, not us. The Bible teaches forgiveness and love. We will do well if we follow that teaching. It may be difficult, but with God's help, we can do this.

Prayer: Lord, help me to forgive and just trust You. It is in Your hands. Help me to be loving and forgiving. Thank You. Amen.

Prayers, Thoughts, Gifts of Joy Today:

APRIL 28

"And Jesus answering saith unto them, 'Have faith in God.' "

-MARK 11:22

What does it mean to have faith? To me, it means to trust and believe—trusting what He says to be true and placing our life in His hands. Often, I trust for a while, and then find myself going my own way, doing what I feel to be right, without praying and asking for direction or help. I trust myself without asking God. When I go in this direction, I usually find consequences to my choices, resulting from my wrong decisions. Having faith in God, being prayed up, and staying in close contact with Him is only a prayer away. Ask for His help today. Trust Him.

Prayer: Lord, I believe and have faith in You. Help me to trust You more. Lead me. Guide me today to make choices in Your Will for my life. Thank You. Amen.

Prayers, Thoughts, Gifts of Joy Today:

APRIL 29

". . . whoso trusteth in the Lord, happy is he."
-PROVERBS 16:20

If you want to be happy, trust in the Lord! It is as simple as that, though we may find it difficult to trust in the Lord and let go of control of our own lives. Ultimately, God is in control, so let it be. Why do we not trust Him? We may be afraid that He wants something for us that we wouldn't want. As a loving Heavenly Father, He wants only the best for us, so why is it that we doubt Him? Human nature, I suppose. God created us with a will and gave us the ability to choose. He wants us to choose to worship, love, and trust Him of our own free will. We will be happy when we do. He tells us very clearly in this verse that if we trust in Him, we will be happy!

Prayer: Lord, thank You for life and for teaching me to trust Your will for my life. Let me trust You more every day. Thank You. Amen.

Prayers, Thoughts, Gifts of Joy Today:

APRIL 30

"Now unto Him that is able to keep you from falling, and to present you faultless before the presence of his glory with exceeding joy, to the only wise God our Saviour, be glory and majesty, dominion and power, both now and ever. Amen."

-JUDE 24-25

How marvelous is this verse. It is our God who is able to keep us until life's end on this earth and then present us before His glory, faultless, because of Christ. Then it says He will do this with "exceeding joy." I love that statement. Oh, how wonderful to know that God, our Savior, will have exceeding joy over us! I will praise Him today because of this.

Prayer: Thank you, Lord, for being my Savior and giving me your scriptures to bless and encourage me. Just reading these verses blesses me today. Thank You. Amen.

Prayers, Thoughts, Gifts of Joy Today:

MAY 1

"And ye shall seek me, and find me, when ye shall search for me with all your heart."
-JEREMIAH 29:13

I f we seek God with all our heart, we will find Him. The verse above gives us this promise. Seeking God—what does this mean? I believe it means to pray and read His Work, wanting to know Him, wanting Him to be involved in our life in every way, giving control of our lives over to Him, and asking Him to guide us in all we do and say. Every morning, look for Him, and ask Him to help you through your day. Watch for Him, and you will find Him.

Prayer: Lord, be with me this day in all I do, all I say, all I am. I want You to be in my life, in every part. Thank You. Amen.

Prayers, Thoughts, Gifts of Joy Today:

". . . when I sit in darkness, the Lord shall be a light unto me."

-MICAH 7:8

In this life, there will be times of trouble. Darkness will come, but we can always know God is right there with us! He will "never leave you or forsake you." He will be our light through the dark night. Do not lose hope, and do not lose sight of His light. Allow His light to shine for us and through us to others. God's light can shine in us and bless others around us. Through our days and nights of darkness (trouble and despair), we can help others because we have been through the darkness and allowed His light to show us the way to the other side.

Prayer: O God of light and love, help me today, and help me to help others with Your love and light. Thank You. Amen.

Prayers, Thoughts, Gifts of Joy Today:

"The Lord bless thee, and keep thee:
The Lord make his face to shine upon thee, and
be gracious unto thee.
The Lord lift up his countenance upon thee,
and give thee peace."

-NUMBERS 6:24-26

To be blessed by the Lord, to have His face shine upon us, and to receive His grace and peace—oh, what a true blessing! Receive His peace and His blessings today. He wants us, His children, to have His peace in our hearts and lives. The above prayer blessing is one we can pray for ourselves, as well as for others. These are beautiful verses from God's Word. Take them into your heart today. Be blessed!

Prayer: Thank You, Lord, for these verses and the blessing of peace. In a world of unrest and stress, I can find peace because of You. Thank You. Amen.

Prayers, Thoughts, Gifts of Joy Today:

MAY 4

"They that trust in the Lord shall be as Mount Zion, which cannot be removed, but abideth forever."

-PSALM 125:1

When we truly trust in the Lord, we cannot be shaken or moved. Our faith and trust should grow deeper and stronger throughout our life. We see what God has done in our past, and we put our trust and hope in Him for our present and future. We will be strong like a mountain. The Lord is our God, our strength, our shield, our refuge in times of trouble. We place our lives in His capable hands.

Prayer: O God, my God, I trust in You today. Lead me, guide me to make right decisions and choices in my life. Give me Your power and wisdom. Give me a calm assurance that You are here with me. Thank You. Amen.

Prayers, Thoughts, Gifts of Joy Today:

"I will both lay me down in peace, and sleep:
for thou, Lord, only makest me dwell in safety."
-Psalm 4:8

Lie down in peace. Don't worry and fret because God is your safety, your guardian, and your protector. Victor Hugo wrote, "Go to sleep in peace. God is awake." We can rest peacefully, without fear, when God is watching over us. We catch ourselves worrying and being afraid when we don't trust God. With God, there is no fear. He is our shield from evil and harm. We can trust Him. We may think, "Well, bad things still happen sometimes." Yes, they do, and we don't always understand why; however, we, like Job, can still trust God. He is in charge of all things. We can let go of control and be at peace.

Prayer: Lord, thank You for being there for me always, for being my protector and keeping me in Your arms. I place my life in Your hands. Thank You. Amen.

Prayers, Thoughts, Gifts of Joy Today:

MAY 6

"The Lord is my shepherd; I shall not want."
-PSALM 23:1

With the Lord before us, leading and guiding us, we shall not want or need anything more. Keeping Him always before us, as our guide, shepherd, and compass is the goal. We often find ourselves off course because we have lost sight of our shepherd or have wandered away. When this happens, we find ourselves going in all directions, roaming around without a clear direction ahead. Stop and pray, when this occurs, asking God to lead us, and He hears. We shall want for nothing when we truly depend on our shepherd. He will lead us to still waters and restore our soul, bless us, and care for us. What a wonderful blessing this is in our lives.

Prayer: Oh Lord, my shepherd, keep me in Your tender watch and care today. Let my eyes be open to see that when I am aware of Your presence, I have real joy, calm, and peace and need nothing more. Thank You. Amen.

Prayers, Thoughts, Gifts of Joy Today:

MAY 7

"I will say of the Lord, he is my refuge and my fortress: my God; in him I trust."

-Psalm 91:2

God takes care of us. He is "our refuge and our fortress"— a hiding place away from the storms of life. Oh, the storms may still come, but we trust in our God to keep us safe through the storm. He will comfort us, hide us, protect us, and see us through. Even when we become afraid, we can call out to Him in prayer; He will hear us and calm our fears. We do not have to go through anything alone because our God is with us. He will not allow circumstances to overwhelm us. He will be our strength when we are weak. I have large oak trees in my yard, and whenever a bad storm comes, I think about them and pray to God to keep me safe and not let them fall on my house and me. Then I go to sleep in peace, knowing that God is in control. And if He allows them to fall, He is still in control, and whatever happens, I will be okay (even if I am crushed and go to heaven)! Again, I think, **"Go to sleep in peace. God is awake." Victor Hugo.**

Prayer: Lord, I take comfort and strength from Your promises to be my refuge and my fortress, a stronghold in times of trouble. I trust You, God. Thank You. Amen.

Prayers, Thoughts, Gifts of Joy Today:

". . . behold, I am with thee, and will keep thee in all places whither thou goest."

-GENESIS 28:15

G od will be with us wherever we may go and keep us when we are His children. Take comfort in this. He knows where we are, our innermost thoughts, and He loves and cares for us. **"Awareness of His presence contains joy that can endure <u>all</u> eventualities." Sarah Young.** When we keep aware of Him, we will never feel alone. This gives such joy and comfort, knowing that we are never alone. He is always with us and keeps us. We can rest and relax in this truth.

Prayer: God, thank You for always being here with me and keeping me in Your loving care. Let me think on this truth and know it even more. I can find great rest and peace in this. Thank You. Amen.

Prayers, Thoughts, Gifts of Joy Today:

MAY 9

"In all thy ways acknowledge him, and he shall direct thy paths."

We need God's guidance in every step we take, in every path we choose. When we acknowledge Him and ask Him to lead and guide us, He will. Stay open to Him and His guidance by staying in close relationship with Him through prayer and Bible study. He will never lead us anywhere contrary to His Word. He will stay faithful and true to us always. When we pray and trust in God, our decisions will come easier to us. His gentle guidance will lead us day by day and moment by moment. Do not rush ahead of God. Be still and quiet and know that He is God. Wait for Him.

Prayer: Lord, I ask You to direct all the paths I take today. Lead me. Guide me in every decision and every choice for I know Your way is right for me. I need Your direction always and in everything. Thank You. Amen.

Prayers, Thoughts, Gifts of Joy Today:

**"In all their affliction, he was afflicted, and the
angel of his presence saved them: in his love and
in his pity he redeemed them; and he bare them,
and carried them all the days of old."**

-ISAIAH 63:9

In God's love and mercy, He will lift us up and carry us all of our days, even unto old age. When we are distressed, suffering, and afflicted, He feels our pain with us and sends His angel to save us. "The angel of His presence"—oh, how I love this line. Just think, God sends an angel to watch over us and to keep us safe! I remember after my David died how sometimes I would weep uncontrollably and feel so alone, distressed, like my world had fallen apart. But every time, it seemed, as I was crying, a warmth would envelop me, and I would just know it was God there with me. I felt He understood how sad and broken I was and was putting His arms around me. Wow! When we are His child, it is wonderful! We are precious in His sight, precious to God, our Heavenly Father. He cares; He really does care when we hurt. We should stand, or rather, fall on our knees in awe of this knowledge. Praise God!

Prayer: O God, my Father, I do stand amazed that You care so much for me, that You are distressed when I am distressed, and care, really care, and send Your angel to comfort me. Thank You. Amen.

Prayers, Thoughts, Gifts of Joy Today:

". . . greater is he that is in you, than he that is in the world."

-1 JOHN 4:4

The Lord God is greater, more powerful, and stronger than Satan and his forces of evil. Some days it may not seem that way, but the Bible tells us this is true, and I believe the Bible. This verse gives me courage, strength, and hope. I have read the end of the world's story and Christians—we win! God, the all-powerful one, wins! When you feel weak, pray and pray again. "Greater is He that is in you. . . ." Tune in to that power, that greatness today, this very minute. He has not given us a spirit of weakness and powerlessness, but one of strength and boldness! Use it for His glory.

Prayer: Lord God, thank You for this verse today. Let me realize the power You have given to me. Let me stand and speak with strength and boldness, with love and kindness always, for my faith and belief in the Lord Jesus Christ. Thank You. Amen.

Prayers, Thoughts, Gifts of Joy Today:

MAY 12

**"Heaviness in the heart of man maketh it stoop:
but a good word maketh it glad."**

-PROVERBS 12:25

Say a good, kind, uplifting word today to lighten someone's heart. We may never know what our kind words and a smile or a hug may do for another's day. Always let kind words— words of encouragement—come from our mouth. Encourage, uplift, and speak peace to those who are in our path today. Look into people's eyes and smile as we meet them. Show them God's love through our care. Make someone glad today. Make someone's day better. What are we here for, if not to lighten someone's load and help them along the way? Helping others is a good way to live, day in and day out.

Prayer: Lord, help me to be a blessing to someone today through my words, my deeds, and my actions. Bless me, O Lord, so that I may bless others. Thank You. Amen.

Prayers, Thoughts, Gifts of Joy Today:

"And whatsoever ye do in word or deed, do all in the name of the Lord Jesus, giving thanks to God and the Father by him."

-COLOSSIANS 3:17

All we do should be to glorify Jesus' name. The words we speak and the deeds we do should bring honor to Him. When we keep this in our minds, we will be inclined to say only kind words and do noble deeds. We will lead good, honest lives if we follow this command or advice for living. Think of Jesus and His Word as we go through this day He has given us. Bless Him as we bless those around us. "May the words of our mouth and the meditation of our heart be acceptable in His sight."

Prayer: May I live today to bless You, O God, with my words and my deeds, my thoughts and my actions. Help me to do the right things in Your name and only bring You glory and honor, never embarrassment or shame. When I do wrong or say wrong things, let me see them immediately and ask Your forgiveness. Thank You. Amen.

Prayers, Thoughts, Gifts of Joy Today:

"The eternal God is thy refuge, and underneath are the everlasting arms. . . ."

-DEUTERONOMY 33:27

Underneath us are His everlasting arms! We should be able to rest in those. Everlasting— they will not fail us or drop us. We can depend and take refuge in them. Eternal, never-ending love is ours through Jesus Christ, our Lord and Savior. What a divine joy this verse is for us today. Jesus promises never to leave us or forsake us. We may pull away from Him, but He will always be there for us. Just call out to Him today in prayer. Relax and enjoy the peace of His presence. We can relax in His arms. He is not going to drop us.

Prayer: Thank You, God, for holding me up, for Your presence and Your strength. I am resting in Your everlasting arms today. Thank You. Amen.

Prayers, Thoughts, Gifts of Joy Today:

MAY 15

**". . . fear not; for I have redeemed thee, I have
called thee by thy name; thou art mine."**

-ISAIAH 43:1

We do not ever have to be afraid because we belong to God. Isn't that great news? Why should we ever worry and fret? We sometimes forget whose we are and who we are—children of the Most High God! Through Him, we have the power to overcome. We are redeemed because of Him in our life. We can hold our head up, walk strong, and "fear not" because He has us in His care. Take strength when we read this verse. We are His child! Rejoice and be happy!

Prayer: Praise to You, God, for I belong to You. I will not fear, for You have redeemed (saved) me! Thank You for Your love, mercy, grace, forgiveness, and acceptance as Your child. I am yours. Amen.

Prayers, Thoughts, Gifts of Joy Today:

"Enter into his gates with thanksgiving, and into his courts with praise; be thankful unto him, and bless his name. For the Lord is good; his mercy is everlasting; and his truth endureth to all generations."

-Psalm 100:4-5

Give God our praise and thank Him every day for His goodness and mercy. Bless Him with our praise continually. Know that He is good. With our worship, praise, and thankfulness, we please Him. Be ever joyful in His presence today. Enter into His presence with a thankful heart. He loves us and has done great things for us. Be ever and always grateful.

Prayer: Lord, thank You for showing me mercy, love, and kindness. I give You all praise, and I worship You today. Thank You for all my blessings. Even when things aren't "perfect" in my life, I am still thankful to You for all You have done and will do. Amen.

Prayers, Thoughts, Gifts of Joy Today:

MAY 17

"Behold, I will do a new thing; now it shall spring forth; shall ye not know it? I will even make a way in the wilderness, and rivers in the desert."

-ISAIAH 43:19

God will make a way where there seems no way. He can do the seemingly impossible for us. He may have something new in store for us. Sometimes new is good—a new thing! We don't always need to cling on so tightly to our old ways, what we are comfortable with. Instead, we should allow God to open new doors, new paths for us. Be open to His Will, what He has in store for us. He can make a way for us, even in our wilderness of despair, and open up rivers of flowing, fresh, clear water in our time in the desert. When we are going through a bad time in our life, we can read this verse and find hope. Change is difficult for us sometimes. Hold on and know that God has our best interest in His plans. Even when we do not understand what is happening in our life and why, we can be assured of this: God loves us and has a good plan for us!!!

Prayer: God, help me to be aware of the new things You have for my life, even in the wilderness and desert. Bring me out and show me Your hope. Thank You. Amen.

Prayers, Thoughts, Gifts of Joy Today:

". . . shine as lights in the world."

-PHILIPPIANS 2:15

S hine our light. Light the way for others to see Jesus in us. God is light, not darkness. Shine, smile, love, care, and do good today. When we do these things, do them as unto the Lord. Watch and pay close attention to our attitude, our words, and deeds because we are an ambassador for Christ in this world. When we are finished here on this earth, may the world say she (he) shined brightly for Christ! Our main purpose in this life is to worship, praise, and glorify God, to be a light for Him, and shine His light to those He places in our way each day. When we understand this and see this as our life's purpose, He can use our lives for His glory and honor. All we do, all we say, all we are can be used by Him to shine out in this world. Shine for Jesus Christ today!

Prayer: Father, let me be Your light today. Keep me bright and shining for You! Thank You for shining through me. May others see Jesus in me today. Guard my words and my deeds so that I never bring dishonor to Your name. Thank You. Amen.

Prayers, Thoughts, Gifts of Joy Today:

MAY 19

"Return unto thy rest, O my soul; for the Lord hath dealt bountifully with thee. For thou hast delivered my soul from death, mine eyes from tears, and my feet from falling."

-PSALM 116:7-8

The Lord has been good to us. We can rest and relax in His love and care over us. We don't have to be afraid or worry about anything. He has delivered us over and over again. Our soul can be at rest because we are His. He holds us in His hand for this life and for all eternity! Praise be to His name. Isn't it a wonderful blessing we are given from God that we can rest in Him? Yes, it is. Let us accept this blessing and praise Him. Knowing this, why is it that we often start worrying and fretting? I don't know. This is just human nature, I suppose. I do it, and I am sure you do as well. Keeping in God's Word helps us with this problem of worrying and fretting. By reading, praying, and keeping in His Word, we are reassured daily that He has this and we shouldn't worry and fret. Okay, let's get this through our heads and hearts!

Prayer: Thank You, Lord, that You have been so good to me and have delivered my soul, dried my tears, and kept me from falling. I praise Your name today. Thank You. Amen.

Prayers, Thoughts, Gifts of Joy Today:

"Jesus Christ the same yesterday, and today, and forever."

-HEBREWS 13:8

We can count on Jesus Christ. He does not change; He is "the same yesterday, and today, and forever." We can put our faith, our hope, and our trust in the ever-constant one, the never changing one! This verse should give us great comfort and great hope. Everything in this life will change and does change—except for Jesus Christ. He is the only one who never changes. He is truth and right, and there is no changing or shadow of wrong with Him. In this world, there are few constants, but Jesus Christ is the true, real constant. When the world around us gets shaken up and things seem to be broken and unfixable, we can rely on Jesus Christ—"the same yesterday, and today, and forever."

Prayer: Thank You, Jesus, for Your power, Your truth, and Your Word. Let it guide me, lead me, and uphold me. Let it be my firm foundation, now and forever. When all around me is shaken up, You are still in control. Let me remember this today. Thank You. Amen.

Prayers, Thoughts, Gifts of Joy Today:

MAY 21

"For, lo, the winter is past, the rain is over and gone; the flowers appear on the earth; the time of the singing of birds is come, and the voice of the turtle is heard in our land."

-Song of Solomon 2:11-12

May is one of my favorite months. Winter is past and the flowers appear. It is glorious! Birdsong sweetens the skies. God has blessed us with spring again. Just as seasons come—spring, summer, autumn, and winter—so it is in our lives. God gives us spring again after the hard, cold winter in our lives. Rejoice and give praise to God, and breathe in the spring air. Remember as you go through life, morning comes again after the night, and spring comes again after the winter. You may go through a difficult time, but God will send the good once again to you. Hang on; spring is coming!

Prayer: God, thank You for spring, for the flowers, the singing of birds; all the wonderful gifts You give to my life. Thank You for the beauty of the earth all around me today. Let me breathe deeply and thankfully. Amen.

Prayers, Thoughts, Gifts of Joy Today:

MAY 22

"These things I have spoken unto you, that in me ye might have peace."

-JOHN 16:33

I have used the second part of this verse earlier. It goes on to say, "In the world, ye shall have tribulation: but be of good cheer (have joy); I have overcome the world." This is a powerful verse. He spoke these words to give us peace, a calm, an assurance. We, as Christians, know who wins in the end. We are also given peace and power, through Jesus Christ, to stand firm in our faith. When we read and study the Word of God, we can find peace in our lives. God is in control, not us. We don't have to worry and fret or be dismayed and distressed because He has us. He will give us peace. Take His peace today.

Prayer: Lord, help me today, in this world of tribulation, to have peace and joy in You. I can get all upset and out of sorts when I listen to the news on TV or in the media, but help me to remember who is really in charge. Thank You. Amen.

Prayers, Thoughts, Gifts of Joy Today:

MAY 23

"For thou art my lamp, O Lord: and the Lord will lighten my darkness."

-2 SAMUEL 22:29

The Lord will bring light to our darkness. How wonderful! What a blessing. He is a lamp, a light in our life so that we might be able to see where we are going, so we don't stumble and fall. A light in a dark room gives us comfort. We don't like to sit in the dark, do we? A light brightens up the space around us and makes us feel more secure. This is what God does for us. He is the light in a dark world. If we follow in His light, He will guide our way. He will lead us to even more light and brighter days.

Prayer: Oh God, thank You for Your light in the darkness. Be close to me today. Shine the way clearly for me. Light my path as I go through this day. Brighten my life with Your love. Let me shine a light to others along my way as well. Thank You. Amen.

Prayers, Thoughts, Gifts of Joy Today:

"The light of the eyes rejoiceth the heart: and a good report maketh the bones fat."

-PROVERBS 15:30

G ood news! Be a bearer of good news today. Give a good, positive word to others to help lift them up. Keep a smile on your face and a light in your eyes; the light of Jesus' love. We will then live in joy and peace when we have Jesus' love in our life. Jesus loves us and wants to give us His light; all we have to do is ask and we will receive. The Bible tells us that Jesus is light; in Him, there is no darkness. When we follow Jesus and His Word, we will live in the light. That doesn't mean there will never be times of darkness in our lives, times of struggle and heartache, but it does mean that we will keep on praying, believing, and asking Him to walk with us through the dark times of our life and lead us toward His light. He is there with us even in the darkness, drawing us toward the light. Today, I was a bit down and discouraged, and all of a sudden, the tune to 'Jesus Loves Me' came into my mind, and I was singing it without even realizing it. This caused me to stop and think that God put this into my mind, reminding me He loves me!

Prayer: Lord, thank You for Your Word, Your light, Your joy today. Help me to keep my eyes on You and Your light. "Thy Word is a light unto my path. . . ." Thank You. Amen.

Prayers, Thoughts, Gifts of Joy Today:

MAY 25

"But I trusted in thee, O Lord; I said, thou art my God. My times are in thy hand: deliver me from the hand of mine enemies, and from them that persecute me."

-PSALM 31:14-15

Our life, our times are in the hand of God. If He is our God, our Savior, we can trust Him to see us through our lives. Pray each morning for His guidance through the day, and He will answer and be there. Keep on keeping on and trust Him. When things don't go as we had planned or hoped, we can still trust Him. He sees and knows things we don't and knows the end of our story. When I was sick and going through a troubled time, there were nights when I woke up, afraid I was dying; a sort of panic attack was going on. When this happened, I prayed and tried to relax and breathe. As I prayed, I realized, "My times are in His hands." If it is time for me to die, I will. I didn't want to die just yet, but I really had no control over it. God has the control over my times. I can relax in this knowledge.

Prayer: Thank You, Lord, for this day, this time You have given me. Let me use the time wisely and bring honor and glory to You in everything I do or say. Thank You. Amen.

Prayers, Thoughts, Gifts of Joy Today:

"Be of good courage, and he shall strengthen your heart, all ye that hope in the Lord."

-PSALM 31:24

God will give us the strength to keep on, when our hope and trust lies in Him. Sometimes life kicks us when we are down, and we are discouraged and beaten up. Let us take hope and courage from verses like this one from God's Word, and get up and go forward with His love and strength for today. He will get us through; I know He will. He promises this to us in His Word. In the Bible, some of His disciples were killed, imprisoned, and went through terrible things. We may think, "Well, He didn't rescue them, did He?" In the world, there have been missionaries—people who were working for the Lord—who have been killed doing His work. I don't understand all of this, and I am sure you don't, but I do believe that God had them in His care and took them on to heaven. Because of what they did, their story led countless to Christ. Often we never know the whole story, or we don't know how one life may have been affected because of their life or their death. We think in terms of this world; God thinks in eternal terms.

Prayer: Lord, give me Your courage and strength today. Hold my hand. Lift me up, I pray. Thank You. Amen.

Prayers, Thoughts, Gifts of Joy Today:

MAY 27

"Go thy way, eat thy bread with joy, and drink thy wine with a merry heart; for God has accepted thy works."

-ECCLESIASTES 9:7

Oh, it is a joyous thing to be pleasing to the Lord. When we live our lives in a way that is pleasing and acceptable to Him, then we can eat in peace with joy and drink with a happy heart. This should be the goal for our life—to live a life acceptable and pleasing to the Lord. Then we can find real joy. How do we do this? Reading God's Word and following its teachings and precepts will lead us to the acceptable and pleasing way. God's Word will never lead us to do wrong. Pray and ask God to help you.

Prayer: O Lord, I want to live today in such a way that is pleasing and acceptable to You. Help me. Lead me to do this. Thank You. Amen.

Prayers, Thoughts, Gifts of Joy Today:

"Yet the Lord will command his loving kindness in the daytime, and in the night his song shall be with me, and my prayer unto the God of my life."

-PSALM 42:8

We have God with us day and night. His loving kindness is with us, and His song is ever in our hearts. God is the God of our life. I love this statement: "Prayer unto the God of my life." He is God of my daytime, God of my night, God of my life. How comforting to know this! Our life must be wrapped up in Him, because He gives us our life. Of course, we have to go about our days and live our lives, but when we put Christ at its center, we can live more alive and fully. He will bless us with a joy and peace beyond the world's understanding. We can know God and know His peace today.

Prayer: Dear Lord, thank You for being with me always, day and night. My prayers go up to You, and You put a song in my heart. Thank You. Amen.

Prayers, Thoughts, Gifts of Joy Today:

"Teach me to do thy will; for thou art my God: thy spirit is good; lead me into the land of righteousness."

-PSALM 143:10

Sometimes it is hard for us to know the real will of God in our lives. We pray and ask but don't find a clear, easily understood answer. We keep praying and seeking His lead in what we are doing, but say, "God, just write it on the wall for me, would You?" We can understand His teachings and know and understand right from wrong, but maybe we aren't really facing an outright wrong—just a decision as to what we should do in a situation, or where we should go, and we aren't getting a clear answer. Life's choices aren't always about just right or wrong, but about good and best sometimes. How do we judge between good and best in our life? Pray, read His Word, and listen to those around us, if we feel they are spiritually minded. Maybe write out the pros and cons on paper and read them over. Does one outweigh the other? Wait on the Lord to give a more clear understanding. Waiting is the hard part, but we shouldn't rush ahead of God.

Prayer: Teach me to do Your will today, Lord. Lead me. Guide my life. Help me to always choose Your way for myself. Keep my mind and heart in Your will, I pray. Thank You.

Prayers, Thoughts, Gifts of Joy Today:

"Above all, taking the shield of faith, wherewith ye shall be able to quench all the fiery darts of the wicked."

-EPHESIANS 6:16

When we trust God and put our faith in Him, He gives us His Spirit within us so that we might be strong enough to overcome evil and wicked all around us in the world. We are blessed because of this. Above all, we should take the shield of faith; hold it up before us as we start each new day. With God's help, we can do this thing called life, and do it well! Yes, we can—with God's help! It isn't always easy to fight against the wicked. We get tired of fighting and want to give up and give in. That is much easier. God asks us to stand firm, to take up the shield of faith and put out the "fiery darts of the wicked." We can do this with God's help; never alone. Remember this: we are never alone.

Prayer: Jesus, help me today to put my faith in You totally, so that I can fight off any wicked or evil that comes at me from the world. Thank You because You make me strong enough. Amen.

Prayers, Thoughts, Gifts of Joy Today:

MAY 31

"Therefore with joy shall ye draw water out of the wells of salvation."

-ISAIAH 12:3

The only real, true joy comes from Jesus Christ and His salvation. We can draw from that well and never thirst again. The Lord can help us think up, be up, look up, and go forward in joy! "The joy of the Lord is my strength" today. In the Lord, we have hope and joy! Be blessed today! Because of whose we are and who we are, we can have joy every day!!! The world may try to get us down, discourage us, dismay us, beat us up, but we can overcome by the power of Jesus Christ in our lives. He will give us joy and a spirit of hope today. Ask for it. Take it and go! The saddest thing is a defeated Christian. We don't have to go about defeated because we have Almighty God on our side.

Prayer: Jesus, thank You for my salvation. Give me Your joy today; the joy that only You can give. Lift me up! Let me stand strong and courageous! Thank You. Amen.

Prayers, Thoughts, Gifts of Joy Today:

JUNE 1

"Then thou shalt call, and the Lord shall answer;
thou shalt cry, and he shall say, here I am."

-ISAIAH **58:9**

"And the Lord shall guide thee continually,
and satisfy thy soul in draught, and make fat
thy bones: and thou shalt be like a watered garden, and like a spring of water, whose waters
fail not."

-ISAIAH **58:11**

Call to the Lord, and He will answer us. He is there. What a blessing to us, His children, that He is there for us when we call! He is the God who created us, and He cares when we cry out to Him. We will not fail because we are His children. Oh, we may have setbacks in life, but ultimately, we will overcome if we hold fast our faith in Jesus and trust in Him. He will never leave us or forsake us. We can know this and trust Him.

Prayer: When I pray to You, Lord, You hear and are there for me. Almighty God, my God, You are with me. How wonderful this is! Thank You. Amen.

Prayers, Thoughts, Gifts of Joy Today:

". . . in quietness and in confidence shall be your strength."

-ISAIAH 30:15

In the quiet times of our lives, we can pray, talk to God, ask Him for confidence and strength to go on, and He will hear us. I like to start my day in the quiet of the early morning with God, prayer, His Word, and other devotional books. This helps me to get a right start to the day. To know God is with us through the day ahead helps us have a confidence and strength that only God's children can have. We have all we need when we start the day with God.

Prayer: Lord, I come to You in the quietness of the early morning, before the world around me gets busy and noisy. I find my strength and my confidence in You. Thank You. Amen.

Prayers, Thoughts, Gifts of Joy Today:

"For ye were sometimes darkness, but now are ye light in the Lord: walk as children of light: for the fruit of the Spirit is in all goodness and righteousness and truth; proving what is acceptable unto the Lord."

-EPHESIANS 5:8-10

Walk in the light, not darkness; goodness, not bad. This is what is acceptable to the Lord—that we walk in goodness, truthfulness, and rightness. In our own strength, we may fail at this, but with God's strength, we can succeed in this life. Walk today in God's light. He will light up our life and give us joy! We need to share His joy and love with others. By sharing God's light and joy with the people we come in contact with daily, this keeps His love going. We are to walk as "children of light," and we are to have the fruit of His Spirit, which is "goodness and righteousness and truth."

Prayer: Help me to walk today in Your light and show Your Spirit of goodness and truth and do what is right. Lead and guide me, Lord, I pray. Thank You. Amen.

Prayers, Thoughts, Gifts of Joy Today:

JUNE 4

"Let us not be weary in well doing: for in due season we shall reap, if we faint not. As we have therefore opportunity let us do good unto all men, especially unto them who are of the household of faith."

-GALATIANS 6:9-10

Treat others as we would like to be treated. Don't grow weary or tired of doing good works because good reaps good. We should do good to everyone, but this verse tells us to especially be good to other Christians. Uphold them in our prayers and care for them. We Christians sin and sometimes mess up, even after we become a Christian. Christian brothers and sisters can hurt one another, and we can have conflict with one another, just as families sometimes have conflict. When this happens, we have to pray even harder because we are to be especially good to those in our church or in our faith. Christians fighting with one another damages the work of the Lord. Others think we should behave in a certain way, what they consider Christians to be. Sometimes we fail. We should always pay close attention to our words, our deeds, and our actions.

Prayer: Lord, let me do good to everyone I meet today. Open my eyes and my heart to others. Let me be a blessing to those whom You put in my path today. Thank You. Amen.

Prayers, Thoughts, Gifts of Joy Today:

JUNE 5

"The Lord is good unto them that wait for him, to the soul that seeketh him."

-LAMENTATIONS 3:25

Seek the Lord in everyday life. Look for Him in all we do, everywhere we go. He is there if we seek Him. The Bible says He will be good to them who wait for Him. What does waiting on the Lord mean? I think it may mean praying, asking God's guidance, and then waiting for His answer. Waiting and knowing His answer is sometimes hard. If we are seeking His will, His guidance, I feel we will know. If we are following His principles as set forth in the Bible, we will more clearly see His will for us. He will never lead us to do anything contrary to what the Bible teaches. Let this be a guideline for us when seeking His will. Pay close attention to what we are doing; ask ourselves "would this be in God's acceptable plan?"

Prayer: Lord, help me to seek You and Your will for my life. Give me wisdom to discern Your will today. Thank You, Lord. Amen.

Prayers, Thoughts, Gifts of Joy Today:

JUNE 6

"I will instruct thee and teach thee in the way which thou shalt go: I will guide thee with mine eye."

-PSALM 32:8

P ray and seek God's guidance, and He will instruct and teach us in the way we should go. We have decisions to make every day. With God's help, we can make wise choices. Know that God will never lead us to do anything wrong. When we study God's Word, we will know right from wrong. His principles never change. They are our guideline. He does not change. He is "the same yesterday, and today, and forever." The world's views change, customs change, people change, but God remains the same. The world tries to confuse us by looking at right and wrong and the "gray areas." We know there are two sides to everything, often more than two; however, God's Word and His principles do not change. Read His Word for yourself and strive to know God. He is the judge, not us; that's for sure. He is a just God and a Holy God whom we do not fully comprehend.

Prayer: Teach me to do Your will, Oh Lord, I pray. Guide me today and watch over me. Thank You for always being here for me, for loving and for caring. Amen.

Prayers, Thoughts, Gifts of Joy Today:

"Rejoicing in hope; patient in tribulation; continuing instant in prayer."

-ROMANS 12:12

We have hope; rejoice in this! We have the greatest hope of heaven throughout eternity. We can, therefore, remain patient in troubles and tribulations because our hope is in God. We should constantly pray because prayer is our gateway to Jesus Christ—our help, our hope, our joy, and salvation. Because of Him, we have great hope always. Rejoice and have hope today! Think up!!! Think joy!!! Think hope!!!

Prayer: God of hope, I rejoice and am glad in You today. You are my salvation and my song of joy. I can think up today because of who You are. Thank You. Amen.

Prayers, Thoughts, Gifts of Joy Today:

> "... lay hold upon the hope set before us: which hope we have as an anchor of the soul, both sure and steadfast...."
>
> **-HEBREWS 6:18-19**

Hope is the anchor of the soul. I love this statement. An anchor holds us in place and keeps us from drifting aimlessly. It makes us sure and steadfast, steady, strong, courageous, and brave. Because we know in whom we believe, we are strong. He gives us the strength to go on day by day. He is our rock, our foundation, and our hope! Without hope, life would be a frightening thing, but with hope, we can face our tomorrows with joyful anticipation and excitement, knowing God has all things in His plan and in His control. We can have great hope in Jesus Christ, the anchor of our soul.

Prayer: Lord Jesus, thank You for being my anchor and holding me fast throughout the storms of life. I know You will not let me drift away but will hold on to me. I put my faith and hope in You. Amen.

Prayers, Thoughts, Gifts of Joy Today:

JUNE 9

"Be ye doers of the word, and not hearers only . . . ."

-JAMES 1:22

Do the words we speak match the way we live? If not, we are a fake. We are to hear the Word of God and apply it to our daily lives—live it in word and in action. If the Word really goes into our heart, we will be a doer of the Word and not just hear it. We have heard it said that "actions speak louder than words." This is so true. What we do speaks loudest. We must live our lives in such a way that others will see we are followers of God's Word, and our lives show that we apply God's teachings daily. We cannot live Godly lives without His help. He promises to help us each day.

Prayer: Today, Lord, let me hear what You have to say to me through reading Your Holy Word, and then help me to live and be a "doer" of Your Word. Thank You. Amen.

Prayers, Thoughts, Gifts of Joy Today:

JUNE 10

"Set your affections on things above, not on things on the earth."

-COLOSSIANS **3:2**

Think up! Think on God and His goodness and glory. We spend so much time worrying about earthly things, we sometimes forget God is in control. Don't worry. Pray. Ask God to help us through this earthly mess, and then rely on Him; set our affections on God. The Bible tells us to "pray without ceasing." This means to pray about everything. We are told to give our burdens to the Lord. We should set our affections, our goals, our life on Him and on doing His will.

Prayer: God, help me to stop worrying and simply put my mind on You. Help me trust and rely on You. Thank You. Amen.

Prayers, Thoughts, Gifts of Joy Today:

JUNE 11

". . . . I will not forget thee."

-ISAIAH 49:15

God promises to never forget us. He promises to always be with us and never leave us alone. No matter what we are going through, He is there. Just call out to Him for help and care. He will never leave us or forsake us—NEVER!!! The Bible tells us so. When we are afraid or feel alone, like the whole world is against us and nothing is going right, we can read this verse and know God said, "I will not forget you." We can trust Him, rely on Him. We can have hope and assurance because of the Word of God.

Prayer: God, thank You for Your love and care, and for never leaving me alone. When I feel alone, remind me that You are here with me through all of this. Thank You for Your promises in Your Word. Amen.

Prayers, Thoughts, Gifts of Joy Today:

JUNE 12

**"For thou hast made him most blessed forever:
thou hast made him exceeding glad. . . ."**

-PSALM 21:6

The Lord can make us joyful and glad. When we are discouraged, sad, and down, we can look up to God. He will bless us and cause us to have exceeding joy again! In His presence, there is joy and gladness. He is near; just call on Him. He is there. When we feel the most sadness, this is just the time we need to call out to Him even more because He wants to bless us and bring us joy. We are His child. He loves us and wants to bless us and bring us exceeding gladness!!!

Today, accept His blessings, His gladness and joy.

Prayer: Lord, be very near me today. Let me find joy and gladness in Your presence. Let me rejoice and be happy because of You. Thank You for caring and being here for me. Amen.

Prayers, Thoughts, Gifts of Joy Today:

JUNE 13

> **"Let no corrupt communication proceed out of your mouth, but that which is good to the use of edifying, that it may minister grace unto the hearers."**
>
> -EPHESIANS 4:29

L et nothing come from our mouths that isn't good or is not life affirming and encouraging. This is a difficult task, isn't it? We are to be gracious, uplifting, encouraging, and the bearers of good news. Every morning, before starting our day, we should pray a prayer asking God to help us not to speak words other than good, uplifting, loving, kind words. This should be our goal every morning as we begin our day. God will help us reach this goal when we ask. When we think on good things, choose good to listen to, to read, to be around; then we can be more assured that we will be more filled with grace and share that grace with others.

Prayer: Lord, guard my mouth and heart today. Let only good, kind, loving, uplifting, encouraging words come from my mouth-words that praise, honor, and glorify You. "May the words of my mouth and the meditations of my heart be acceptable in Your sight." Use my mouth to glorify You and bring joy and encouragement to others. Thank You. Amen.

Prayers, Thoughts, Gifts of Joy Today:

JUNE 14

"... my heart shall not fear ... in this will I be confident."

-PSALM 27:3

Because we have Almighty God as our Savior and Redeemer, we should not be afraid. We should be confident, strong, and have courage. Then why do we become afraid? Because we take our eyes off God and start looking around, listening to others, right? When we keep our eyes on Jesus and our mind on Him and His Word, we will grow to trust Him more. His Word tells us over and over to trust Him, not to fear, that He loves us, cares about us, and never will leave us or forsake us. Believe Him. Trust. Do not fear. Find confidence in Him.

Prayer: Lord, I can be confident and not fear because of You. The problems that are coming at me today are frightening, but I know You are with me until the very end of my life and then will take me to heaven. All is well, and all will be well. Thank You, Lord. Amen.

Prayers, Thoughts, Gifts of Joy Today:

JUNE 15

**"Rest in the Lord, and wait patiently for him:
fret not thyself."**

-PSALM 37:7

Rest and trust in the Lord. He can handle things, whatever they may be. Waiting patiently —now that is a hard one for me. How about you? I am trying to learn to do this. Rushing about doesn't help. We can't fix anything ourselves apart from God. The Bible tells us not to fret; don't worry! This is a great verse to read every single day. Before we go out our door for the day or before we even put our feet on the floor in the morning, this verse memorized and repeated, taken into our very heart, is good advice. Don't go around fretting and worrying needlessly. It is going to be all right! Really! God has this!

Prayer: Lord, help me to relax and rest in You today, to trust You, to wait for You, and to stop worrying. Thank You for taking care of me and my problems today. Amen.

Prayers, Thoughts, Gifts of Joy Today:

JUNE 16

"Yet I will rejoice in the Lord, I will joy in the God of my salvation."

-HABAKKUK 3:18

The verse prior to this one said "although," and it listed all these awful things. Although all this happens, "Yet I will rejoice in the Lord." In other words, no matter what happens, "I will joy in the God of my salvation." No matter what is going on in our lives, we should rejoice and have joy in our Lord. Praise His name forevermore! Sometimes it is hard to praise the Lord and rejoice when things around us are going wrong, when everything seems to be crumbling and caving in around us, when our world is shattered and falling apart. This is just the time to call on the Lord to help us, to bring us through and out on the other side, to give us joy again after the night of crying. Keep on praising God and looking for the joy!

Prayer: Lord, I rejoice in You right now, right this minute, even when things aren't going right and my world seems shattered. You can bring me joy and rejoicing again. Let me keep looking to You, praising You, no matter what. Thank You. Amen.

Prayers, Thoughts, Gifts of Joy Today:

JUNE 17

". . . rejoice in hope of the glory of God."
-ROMANS 5:2

Have hope and rejoice! Christians have hope because of our salvation. God gives us His Spirit to live within us. Therefore, we have great hope! We are to rejoice, sing, be happy and joy-filled because we have His promise to always be with us, to love, care, guide, and go with us every step of our way on this earth and from here into eternity. We have the promise of heaven He has prepared for us. "Rejoice in hope of the glory of God."

Prayer: Dear Jesus, thank You for hope in this life. Thank You for giving me joy and the promise of eternal life with You in heaven. Amen.

Prayers, Thoughts, Gifts of Joy Today:

JUNE 18

"Now the Lord of peace himself gives you peace always by all means. The Lord be with you."
-II THESSALONIANS 3:16

P ray for the Lord to give us peace. He can give a peace that no one else or nothing else can give, a "peace that passes understanding." He talks about peace often in the Bible. He wants us to have peace, to receive peace from Him. The world can get us in turmoil, have us running in every direction, stressed and upset, but God can give us peace if we ask and allow Him to quiet and still our mind and our body. Only Jesus can give a peace that will satisfy and last. Only Jesus can quiet the storms of doubt and fear. Only Jesus can help—really help! Let Him today. Give it all over to Him: worries, fears, doubts, troubles, everything.

Prayer: Lord, give me Your peace and calm in my soul today. Let me feel Your calm come over me. Take it all. Take the stress and hurt from my shoulders and fill me with Your peace and calm. Fill my soul with Your Spirit, Your sweet, Holy Spirit. Thank You. Amen.

Prayers, Thoughts, Gifts of Joy Today:

"Thy word is a lamp unto my feet, and a light unto my path."

-PSALM 119:105

The Lord will light our path for us and guide us by His Holy Word. Read the Bible. It is a guidebook. Its principles will show us how to live a right life. Read and apply the words to daily life. Pray for wisdom and guidance, and then live on this path. He will guide our feet with His light. Stay away from darkness. Stay away from people and things that bring us down. We may not be able to get away from people who bring us down. They may be in our home or at our place of work. We may have to rethink the way we respond to them and readjust our attitudes and responses. Pray. God will help us with this. Stay in His shining light.

Prayer: May I listen always to You and stay on the path of light. Help me to follow You, Lord. Let me rethink my actions, my attitudes, and my responses today to people who bring darkness into my life. Thank You for leading me. Thank You for keeping me in Your light. Amen.

Prayers, Thoughts, Gifts of Joy Today:

JUNE 20

"My flesh and my heart faileth; but God is the strength of my heart, and my portion for ever."
-PSALM 73:26

Our bodies will fail us eventually, as we grow older. It is a certainty that each of us will face if we live a long life. God can be the strength of our hearts, even if our earthly hearts fail. He is enough, our portion forever. He will never fail us. He will go with us all the days of our lives, and take us to Heaven when our time on earth is over. There we will be with Him forever. There He will continue to be our portion!

Prayer: Thank You, Lord, for blessing me today with this verse. My heart and my strength may fail, but You will never fail me. You will be my portion forever. Amen.

Prayers, Thoughts, Gifts of Joy Today:

JUNE 21

"The statutes of the Lord are right, rejoicing the heart. . . ."

-P<small>SALM</small> 19:8

The principles, the precepts, the truth of the Lord are right. When we follow the Word of the Lord, we will live right and this will make us happy. To follow the Lord's ways will give us a happier, fulfilled life because we will be in His care. To live a life in His will brings us true joy. If we want to be happy—and who doesn't—we will follow the truth of the Lord, His principles, and statutes because they are good and right. It sounds so simple, and it is.

Prayer: Oh Lord, help me to follow Your right ways. Help me to make wise decisions today in everything I do, say, and where I go. Be very close and guide me. Thank You. Amen.

Prayers, Thoughts, Gifts of Joy Today:

JUNE 22

"Thou art my hiding place; thou shalt preserve me from trouble; thou shalt compass me about with songs of deliverance."

-PSALM 32:7

God is our place of comfort when troubled. He will give us safety in a hiding place of protection and make us feel secure. He will save us and keep us in His loving care. We can sing songs of praise and deliverance because He has us safely by the hand all the way through this life. When we find ourselves becoming worried or stressed about anything, look at this verse and memorize it so we can recall it quickly, as it will comfort us in times of trouble. So many scriptures are great to memorize to recall so they can help us in the world.

Prayer: Oh God, keep me safely in Your arms this day. Let me feel Your love and care as You watch over me. Let me hide my worries and fears in Your capable hands and leave them there. Thank You. Amen.

Prayers, Thoughts, Gifts of Joy Today:

JUNE 23

"Be glad in the Lord, and rejoice, ye righteous: and shout for joy, all ye that are upright in heart."

-PSALM 32:11

We can be glad, or happy, in the Lord and rejoice when we are made righteous (worthy and good) because of Him. When we accept Jesus Christ as our Savior, we are made clean and righteous because of Him—not because of anything we have done. As followers and believers, we try to walk upright and do good to bring honor and glory to His name. We have joy and gladness in our hearts when His Spirit is within us. Our lives are made better by His love.

Our lives sometimes get all messed up as we live life, but He can put all things right again when we ask Him. We can be glad in the Lord again. Just come to Him today and ask.

Prayer: Lord, let me be glad and shout for joy and be upright in my heart because of my love for You. Thank You for the joy You have given me. Amen.

Prayers, Thoughts, Gifts of Joy Today:

JUNE 24

**"For thou, Lord, wilt bless the righteous; with
favor wilt thou compass him as with a shield."**
-PSALM 5:12

The Lord will surround us with His shield and protect and bless us when we put our faith and trust in Him. This doesn't mean we will never have any problems, but it does mean He will shield and protect us, go with us, and help us. The Lord blesses and keeps us in His loving care daily. Even when we have difficulties and problems in our life, He is there right beside us, holding our hand and keeping us in His care. Don't give up. Keep on keeping on because the Lord is with us. He is on our side. When we try to do right and trust in God, He will be all around us with His shield.

Prayer: Thank You, Lord, for blessing me today and for being a shield against the problems of the world. I can rely on You to always help me face things and to keep on keeping on. Because of You, I can be strong. Thank You. Amen.

Prayers, Thoughts, Gifts of Joy Today:

**"Jesus said, 'I am come that they might have life,
and that they might have it more abundantly.' "**
-JOHN 10:10

Abundant life. What is this? I would say this would be a life of plenty, having an ample, lavish, abounding, bountiful, generous, full life. These are all good adjectives. An abundant life is a good life, filled with plenty, overflowing with abundance. The Bible speaks not of material things, but more importantly, it talks of spiritual blessings from God— an abundance of love, joy, peace, comfort—things money can't buy. Jesus wants to give us this kind of life. He came so that we might enjoy a life like this. Isn't that good news? Oh yes, it certainly is! When we don't have this kind of life, it is not because Jesus fails us and doesn't want us to have this. We can find these abundant life attributes even when we are going through difficulties in our lives because God will give us peace, calm, joy, and comfort—all these abundant life qualities—and be with us no matter what is going on in our life.

Prayer: Jesus, You said You came to give us life, and more abundantly. I thank You today for offering me this abundance. Help me to find it more fully, to watch for and accept Your help and comfort today. Thank You. Amen.

Prayers, Thoughts, Gifts of Joy Today:

JUNE 26

"If I take the wings of the morning, and dwell in the uttermost parts of the sea; even there shall thy hand lead me, and thy right hand shall hold me."

-PSALM 139:9-10

God is with us no matter where we go. He will hold our hand and help us. We should keep trusting; keep on trusting! He will never leave us or forsake us. Believe and receive His love. I love all the verses in the Bible that tell us He holds our hand. It tells us this over and over. When we walk with someone and hold their hand, it means, one, that we care for them, and two, that we help them not to fall and hurt themselves. If they do stumble and fall, we help them get back up by holding their hand. God does this for us. He helps us not to fall or stumble, and if we do fall, He is there to help us up again.

Prayer: Thank You, Lord, for holding my hand and being beside me as I walk through this day before me. It is wonderful and comforting to know You are with me, holding my hand. Amen.

Prayers, Thoughts, Gifts of Joy Today:

> ". . . God of Israel, there is no God like thee, in heaven above, or earth beneath, who keeps covenant and mercy with thy servants that walk before thee with all their hearts."
>
> **-I KINGS 8:23**

There is no God like the one God—the true and living God who has mercy on us and keeps His promises. When we walk with Him, pray to Him, and ask for His goodness, mercy, and grace, He hears and answers. We should walk and talk with Him today as we go about our day. He is there for us in everything. We don't just have to go to Him with the big issues of our life, but go to Him with everything that matters to us. He will hear. Oh, how marvelous!

Prayer: Lord, be near me today as I go about my day. Lead me. Guide my steps. Keep my mind on You. Keep my heart pure. Thank You. Amen.

Prayers, Thoughts, Gifts of Joy Today:

> "Fear ye not therefore, ye are of more value than many sparrows."
> "Are not two sparrows sold for a farthing? And one of them shall not fall on the ground without your Father. But the very hairs on your head are all numbered."
>
> -MATTHEW 10:29-31

God, the Almighty God, is the one who created us, loves us, and cares for us. The Bible tells us He watches us and has even numbered the hairs on our head. We should not be afraid when we trust Him. We may be going through a tough time, but He is there with us, helping us to grow and become the person He wishes us to become. We are of great worth to Him. Imagine that! We are of value to God. This is amazing to think about, isn't it? That the very God of all the world cares about me and knows everything there is to know about me—even the number of hairs I have on my head! My life matters. I matter. Wow!

Prayer: Dear Lord, thank You for caring and being with me today. Thank You that You, the Almighty Holy God, know me and even know the number of hairs on my head. Amazing! Thank You. Amen.

Prayers, Thoughts, Gifts of Joy Today:

JUNE 29

". . . joy, and rejoice with me."

B e happy and rejoice because God has given life to us today and goes with us through this day. All things may not go perfectly, but know that God is ultimately in control, and know that we are loved by Him. The Bible tells us so. No matter what is going on around us, He loves us and cares. Have joy and rejoice! Keep on going. Keep on loving. Keep on praying. Keep on having hope!

Prayer: Thank You, Lord, for Your love and care for me. Because of You, I can have joy and rejoice today. Amen.

Prayers, Thoughts, Gifts of Joy Today:

JUNE 30

"Seek the Lord, and his strength: seek his face evermore."

-PSALM 105:4

If we seek the Lord, we will find Him. He will reveal Himself to us. When we seek the Lord and depend upon His strength instead of our own, we will be more calm and at peace. His strength will be sufficient for us. His calm and peace will keep us still. We should look for Him today in our world. Ask for His help, His guidance, and wisdom. Be still and seek His face. How do we seek the Lord? Prayer, reading our Bible, asking Him to help us and be more active in our lives; these are ways in which we can seek Him. Try to get to know the Lord by reading His Word and finding out more about Him. Find out His character, His attributes, His wishes for us, what His Word tells us of Him. In these ways, we can come to know Him more fully and gain strength from knowing Him.

Prayer: When all around me there may be chaos and strife, You are my calm, my strength, and my joy. Thank You, Lord. I really want to know You more. Amen.

Prayers, Thoughts, Gifts of Joy Today:

JULY 1

"Because thou hast been my help, therefore in the shadow of thy wings will I rejoice."

-PSALM 63:7

If we will look back on our life, we can see how the Lord has helped us over and over again. We can then rest in the knowledge that He will keep on helping us throughout our days. We can and should rejoice in this and give Him our praise and thanks every day of our life. Because He has been our help—and will continue to be our help always—we can rejoice and be glad.

Prayer: Lord, thank You for being my help and for giving me rest in the shadow and shelter of Your arms. I will give You praise and rejoice today. Amen.

Prayers, Thoughts, Gifts of Joy Today:

JULY 2

"Wherefore seeing we also are compassed about with so great a cloud of witnesses, let us lay aside every weight, and the sin which doeth so easily beset us, and let us run with patience the race that is set before us, looking unto Jesus, the author and finisher of our faith . . . lest we become wearied and faint in our minds."

-HEBREWS 12:1-3

If we look to Jesus, and not at those things all around us, we can keep going and not become weary, down, and discouraged. Witnesses—people who have gone before us who taught us and showed us the right way—these tell us to lay aside the things that weigh us down and look to Jesus and live! What weighs us down today? Is it people, or things, or both? We become so busy rushing and hurrying, carrying problems and burdens God doesn't want us to bear, things that weigh heavily on us. These weigh us down under their load. God wants us to lay aside every weight, every burden, every care, and the sins that so easily get us down. He wants us to ask Him to take these burdens from our back and lighten our load. He wants us to give our burdens to Him.

Prayer: Lord, help me today to fix my eyes upon You, only You, so that I do not become weary or lose heart. Keep me "thinking up" and looking up. Thank You. Amen.

Prayers, Thoughts, Gifts of Joy Today:

"The grace of our Lord Jesus Christ be with you."

-1 CORINTHIANS 15:23

Grace: "The free and unearned favor of God!" We did nothing to earn His favor. We don't deserve His favor, yet when we put our faith and trust in Jesus Christ, we receive His grace. Oh, how marvelous! To think that the God of heaven, who created all things, would care and love us is a wonderful and exciting blessing—a blessing we should welcome and receive today. As we go through this day, pray this blessing for others who come into our day. Bless them.

Prayer: Thank You, Lord Jesus, for Your mercy and grace to me today. May I receive Your grace and then show grace to others. Amen.

Prayers, Thoughts, Gifts of Joy Today:

JULY 4

"Blessed is the nation whose God is the Lord. . . ."

-PSALM 33:12

God has blessed us over and over again throughout history, yet we, like nations before us, have not put our God above other gods of money, power, comfort, and values. We fail Him and let Him down. Let us reaffirm today—this very day—our allegiance to our God. Trust in Him to bless our nation. Pray every day for our nation, its leaders, and for ourselves to put Him first, above all else.

Prayer: Thank You, God, for having mercy on us and keeping us in Your care. Help us to put You above all things and trust You. God bless us so that we may bless You!

Prayers, Thoughts, Gifts of Joy Today:

JULY 5

"For whatsoever things were written aforetime were written for our learning, that we through patience and comfort of the scriptures might have hope."

-ROMANS **15:4**

We, as Christians, have great hope. Hope is a feeling of great expectation and trust. Definitions I found when I Googled the word hope were "grounds for believing that something good will happen" and "a person who may help or save someone." These are all good definitions. We have hope in Christ our Lord. We have hope through the scriptures that were written in times past. When we read the scriptures we are given more hope. We can take hold of this hope that is set before us. The problems of life cannot carry us away when we hold on to the hope of God!

Prayer: Thank You, Lord, for hope and Your assurance given to me through Your Word. Amen.

Prayers, Thoughts, Gifts of Joy Today:

JULY 6

"Why art thou cast down, O my soul? And why art thou disquieted in me? Hope thou in God: for I shall yet praise him for the help of his countenance."

-PSALM 42:5

Sometimes we are down and discouraged. Our spirit may be unsettled and upset. The answer to these problems is hope in God. Praise Him. Pray to Him, and He will lift us up, quiet our spirit, and restore our hope. Hope is a wonderful, blessed gift to us. Sometimes we pray, we ask, and yet we do not always get the immediate answer we want. This does not mean God isn't hearing us or listening. He answers. Just because we don't always get what we want does not mean God doesn't care about us and our prayers. Remember, He sees the whole picture of our lives, not just the here and now. There are sometimes more people involved in our prayers than just us, and God sees all of us, not just one person. Our prayers are often selfish and self-centered. If God gave a "yes" to everyone's prayers, this world would be in an awful mess, wouldn't it? When we pray, let us pray in a hopeful, yet unselfish, way and always ask for God's will—not just ours.

Prayer: Lord, thank You for giving me hope today. Lift me up. Quiet my spirit. Restore my hope. I praise You today and give You thanks always for Your guidance. Amen.

Prayers, Thoughts, Gifts of Joy Today:

**". . . your Father knoweth what things ye have
need of before ye ask him."**

-**MATTHEW 6:8**

God knows us. We cannot hide anything from Him or
fake and pretend to Him. He made us. He knows us,
and He knows what we need before we even pray. We often
pray for the wrong things. Our wants may not be in our best
interest. When we pray, we should always ask if it is His will
because He knows—really knows—what is best for us. We
should learn to depend on and trust Him.

Prayer: God, I trust in You. Give me what is best for me
today. Guide my prayers and help me to make wise decisions in all I ask and all I do. Thank You for hearing me
always. Amen.

Prayers, Thoughts, Gifts of Joy Today:

JULY 8

> ". . . He was moved with compassion on them,
> because they fainted, and were scattered abroad,
> as sheep having no shepherd."
>
> -MATTHEW 9:36

God sees and has compassion. When He sees us distressed and downcast, running, scattered in all directions, He cares and has concern for us. He is the Great Shepherd, and we are His sheep. He wants to keep us safe from harm. He wants us to be safe inside His fold. Read the 23rd Psalm. "The Lord is my shepherd; I shall not want . . . He restores my soul . . . ." This is what He wants for us.

Prayer: Lord, "I will fear no evil for Thou are with me" today. Thank You for being with me, for caring, for taking care of me. Amen.

Prayers, Thoughts, Gifts of Joy Today:

> ". . . to give them beauty for ashes, the oil of joy for mourning, the garment of praise for the spirit of heaviness: that they might be called trees of righteousness, the planting of the Lord, that he might be glorified."
>
> -ISAIAH **61:3**

He will turn our sadness, mourning, heaviness, and heartache into joy, praise, and beauty. Things may be bad for us in this moment. We may be going through a difficult time, but we can know that God is there with us through it all. He knows our heartbreak, and He cares. Keep on praying. Keep on going. Ask the Lord to help us through; He will turn our sorrow into joy again. He wants us to be strong in Him and glorify Him in all we do. Give Him the glory!

Prayer: Lord, help me to find beauty, joy, and praise even in the midst of ashes, mourning, and heaviness. I will trust in You and praise You, Lord. Thank You. Amen.

Prayers, Thoughts, Gifts of Joy Today:

JULY 10

"... be strong in the Lord, and in the power of his might."

-EPHESIANS 6:10

We can find our strength in the Lord. He will give us the power to walk daily through life when we rely on Him. There are struggles in this life, but when we turn to Jesus for help, pray, and trust Him, He will be there for us and help us. He will give us the power and strength we need for this very hour. His Word promises this to us. Believe and receive.

Prayer: Lord, I depend on You. Give me the strength and power to go through this day with joy, depending on You. I know with You, all things are possible. Thank You. Amen.

Prayers, Thoughts, Gifts of Joy Today:

"My prayer is 'That he would grant you, according to the riches of his glory, to be strengthened with might by his Spirit in the inner man; that Christ may dwell in your hearts by faith; that ye, being rooted and grounded in love, may be able to comprehend with all saints what is the breadth, and length, and depth, and height; And to know the love of Christ, which passeth knowledge, that ye might be filled with all the fullness of God.' "

-EPHESIANS 3:16-19

K nowing the love of Christ will give us knowledge, strength, and comprehension. The above verses are a wonderful prayer to pray. We want to be "strengthened by His Spirit." We want Christ to dwell in our hearts, to be rooted and grounded in love. The Bible tells us that others will know we are Christians by our love. Hopefully, we will live in such a way that others can see Christ's love flowing out of us. Sometimes we Christians mess up and others cannot see Christ's love in us. We occasionally get off track. When we do, we need to acknowledge it, ask God, ourselves, and others for forgiveness, and then do better. Strive to show God's love as we go about our days and "be filled with all the fullness of God."

Prayer: God, help me today to show your love to others as I go about my day. Guide me, I pray. Keep the words I speak and the deeds I do in Your Will. Gently nudge me when I am going astray and guide me back to You. Fill me with Your fullness, Oh God. Thank You. Amen.

Prayers, Thoughts, Gifts of Joy Today:

JULY 12

"The book of the law shall not depart out of thy mouth; but thou shalt meditate therein day and night, that thou mayest observe to do according to all that is written therein: for then thou shalt make thy way prosperous, and then thou shalt have good success."

-JOSHUA 1:8

The above verse tells us the secret of success and how to be prosperous. It says that if we think on the Word of God, read it, study it, keep it in our hearts and minds and do what it says, we will be prosperous and have good success. I find the words "good success" to be especially meaningful. There are those in this world who have success as the world sees success, but it isn't just and good. I want to have "good success," don't you? Write down what you perceive "success" to be. What is your definition? Compare that to God's principles and see if it adheres to the world's idea of success or God's "good success" in mind for your life. We might want to rethink our idea of success.

Prayer: Lord, help me to live for You, to prosper and have "good success." You know what success is, Lord, more than I do. The world's definition of success is not always Your definition. Help me to know the difference and to choose Your ways. Thank You. Amen.

Prayers, Thoughts, Gifts of Joy Today:

JULY 13

"Yet he liveth by the power of God. For we also are weak in him, but we shall live with him by the power of God."

-2 Corinthians 13: 4

As Christians, we have the power of God in our lives, but we sometimes forget this and are weak and insecure. When we are weak, we can ask God to help us, to give us His strength and power. We sometimes, in our weakness, make wrong decisions. Always know that God is only a prayer away. He will help us to start again. He will forgive if we ask Him. He can turn the wrong around, forgive, and give us His love and power to go again. Trust Him today.

Prayer: I pray for Your power and strength today, Lord. When I feel weak and insecure, You are strong. Help me to rely on Your strength. Thank You. Amen.

Prayers, Thoughts, Gifts of Joy Today:

JULY 14

"Which doeth great things and unsearchable marvelous things without number: who giveth rain upon the earth, and sendeth waters upon the fields: to set up on high those that be low; that those which mourn may be exalted to safety."

-JOB 5:9-11

Our God does great things, wondrous things, such as sending rain. He made us and the world in which we live. When we are low and feeling bad, mourning or in distress, He can lift us up and set us on high places. Think on God, our personal, loving God. Think of His wonder, His power, His might. Let Him lift us today. Ask Him to lift us from our distress, worry, and fear. He will.

Prayer: God, I come to You now recognizing Your power, Your wonder, Your might. Lift me to high places in my spirit now. Let me have joy rather than sadness, strength rather than fear. Thank You. Amen.

Prayers, Thoughts, Gifts of Joy Today:

"And above all things have fervent charity among yourselves: for charity shall cover the multitude of sins. Use hospitality one to another without grudging. As every man hath received the gift, even so minister the same on to another, as good stewards of the manifold grace of God."

-1 PETER 4:8-10

Each of us should use whatever gifts we have been given by God to serve and minister to others. Charity is often translated as love. We are encouraged to love others, to show them hospitality, and to use our talents, our gifts to help others. What gifts or talents do you have? Whatever they are, they can be used to help others, to show love to others. Pray for God to open doors and to show us how to use our gifts for His glory.

Prayer: Lord, open my eyes and heart to see the needs of others and to then use my gifts and talents to help them. Let me be willing to do this. Thank You. Amen.

Prayers, Thoughts, Gifts of Joy Today:

JULY 16

"But the mercy of the Lord is from everlasting to everlasting upon them that fear him, and his righteousness unto children's children."

-PSALM 103:17

God's promise to us, if we reverence Him (respect and revere Him), is that He will make things right and will have mercy on us and our children and grandchildren. This is a wonderful promise. To fear (reverence) Him means we will live our lives according to His teachings. The Bible often talks about fearing God. This doesn't mean we are afraid of Him, but rather that we respect and stand in awe of Him. We do fear His mighty power and should be humble before Him because of who He is—the Almighty God. This is not a bad thing, like we think fear is, but a respectful, honoring type of feeling toward Him. I loved my earthly father and knew he loved me. I was never fearful of him because I knew he loved me and wanted only my best, but I did have a respectful fear of him if he was displeased with my behavior. I knew he would punish me when I disobeyed his rules. This was for my own good, not because he wanted to punish me. He was loving and merciful often, and I didn't always get what I deserved, thank goodness! God, our Heavenly Father, doesn't always give us what we deserve, either.

Prayer: I trust Your Word, Lord, and I keep praying for my children and grandchildren (my loved ones). Have mercy on us and bless us, I pray. Thank You. Amen.

Prayers, Thoughts, Gifts of Joy Today:

JULY 17

"O give thanks unto the Lord, for he is good: because his mercy endureth forever."

-PSALM 118:1

The Lord is good to us and shows us mercy—not giving us what we deserve. He shows us compassion and forgiveness. We should thank Him daily for His great mercy on us. We should show Him our thankfulness by the way we live, the way we go about each precious day He has given us to enjoy. We should keep pleasing Him foremost in our minds and hearts as we go about our day. When we think in this way, we will be in His will.

Prayer: Thank You, Lord, for Your compassion and mercy toward me. You are so good to me. You give me blessings beyond measure. Let me be more aware of all You do for me and be always thankful. Amen.

Prayers, Thoughts, Gifts of Joy Today:

JULY 18

". . . and having done all, to stand."

-**EPHESIANS 6:13**

D o the best you can with God's help, and then stand. Stop; do no more. Let God handle it. Leave it to Him. He can do more than we could ever do alone. With God, all things are possible. When we pray and ask for His help, we can expect miracles. God is there for us. He will help us. The Bible tells us in the above verse to do all we can. God does expect us to do something, not to just pray and sit back and do nothing. We need to ask for God's guidance to lead us to do all we can.

Prayer: God, help me know when to "do" and when to "stop doing" and let You handle it for me. Give me wisdom here. Thank You. Amen.

Prayers, Thoughts, Gifts of Joy Today:

"When thou said, Seek ye my face; my heart said unto thee, thy face, Lord, will I seek."

-PSALM 27: 8

The Lord wants us to strive to know Him, to look for Him, to read His Word, and to get to know Him more. By doing this, our lives will be more content, and we will have less worry and stress because we will trust Him more as we know Him more. We will have more peace in our hearts and find true joy. It isn't always easy to see God's will for our life, is it? When we question and wonder what to do, sometimes the only answer comes from reading God's Word, knowing His principles, and then going forward to do what we feel the "right" Godly thing is in this situation. The answers are not always easy. There may not be a clear right and wrong in our question to God. When we pray honestly to God, asking for His help, He will help us to discern what His will is for us in this time and in this situation. Sometimes the answer may be to "wait." Seeking Him in all we do is the best choice for our lives.

Prayer: Lord, I seek Your face today. When I seek You, I find peace, love, and joy. Thank You. Amen.

Prayers, Thoughts, Gifts of Joy Today:

JULY 20

". . . to be spiritually minded is life and peace."
-ROMANS 8:6

When we set our minds on God, think on Him, we will be able to feel more secure, more at peace, calmer, and less stressed. Think on His Word, read it, and meditate on His promises and His instructions. He tells us how to live freely and fully, if we will listen. We can trust our lives to Him. The Bible is our guidebook to a full and happy life. God created us. He wants us to have joy and peace. The Bible tells us this.

Prayer: Lord, help me today to pay attention to You, to think on You! Give me Your peace, Your calm so that I may feel Your love and thereby be calmed and unstressed. Thank You. Amen.

Prayers, Thoughts, Gifts of Joy Today:

JULY 21

"The name of the Lord is a strong tower: the righteous runneth into it, and is safe."

-PROVERBS 18:10

We can always run to God for help and protection. His name is a place of protection. We are safe in His arms. Run to Him today. Allow Him to save us from whatever it is that hurts us. He is a safe place for our soul, weary and worn though it may be. This verse is a balm of comfort to me in times of turmoil in my life. I call out to the Lord; He hears me and helps me. I will say aloud, "Lord Jesus, help me. I call on Your name right now to help me." I feel a peace, a calm, and His comfort to me when I do this.

Prayer: Lord, my strength and my refuge, I come to You, trusting You with my life. Help me this day. Shield me from harm. Keep me safely in Your arms. Thank You. Amen.

Prayers, Thoughts, Gifts of Joy Today:

JULY 22

**". . . bringing into captivity every thought to the
obedience of Christ."**

-2 CORINTHIANS 10:5

What we think we become, so we must guard our minds
and bring every thought, emotion, and impulse under
the scrutiny of Christ's teachings. Read the Bible, pray, and
ask God for guidance. Look at everything with Christ's principles in mind. When we do this, we can live life more fully
in His will. We have the capacity to control our own thinking
by what we put into our minds every day. How do we begin
our day? What do we read? What do we listen to? To whom
do we listen? We are responsible for guarding our thoughts.
If we have Christ as our center, then we will be much more
protective and watchful of our thoughts.

Prayer: I pray for wisdom and Your guidance, Lord. Help
me to keep my thoughts and actions under Your control
and live rightly. Thank You for helping me through this day.
Amen.

Prayers, Thoughts, Gifts of Joy Today:

JULY 23

"Let us hold fast the profession of our faith, without wavering; (for he is faithful that promised)."

-HEBREWS 10:23

Our God is faithful. Some definitions of the word faithful on Google are "loyal, constant, staunch, steadfast, resolute." Webster says, "Faithful implies unswerving adherence to the oath or promises." Another definition says, "True, devoted, dependable, long-continued, not changing." God promises in His Word to never leave us or forsake us. He is a steady and firm foundation for our lives. We can trust Him.

Prayer: Thank You, God, for Your truth, Your love, Your protection, and Your faithfulness to me. Always. Amen.

Prayers, Thoughts, Gifts of Joy Today:

July 24

"Blessed be the Lord, who daily loadeth us with benefits, even the God of our salvation."

-Psalm 68:19

Day after day, He gives us benefits (blessings). He loads us down with them. We need to pay attention to all He does for us and be thankful and bless Him. Praise Him every day for the blessings He gives us. In my book, *Little Gifts of Joy*, I wrote about looking for and finding the gifts of joy God gives us every day, writing them down, and keeping a journal or log of them. This is a good way in which to notice and then give thanks to God for all of His benefits: gifts, blessings, and joys. When we are aware and appreciative of our blessings, we see even more coming our way. And when we see our blessings, we tend to try to share blessings with those around us and become more generous and giving of ourselves. A thankful, appreciative person is a more giving, loving person.

Prayer: Thank You, Lord, for all You give us every day. Your blessings are new every morning. Great is Your faithfulness to us! Great is Your salvation! Amen.

Prayers, Thoughts, Gifts of Joy Today:

JULY 25

**"For the Lord is our defense; and the Holy One
of Israel is our king."**

-PSALM **89:18**

The very Lord God Almighty is our defense. He defends us and keeps us in His care and safety. We can and should count on Him. This doesn't mean that nothing bad will ever happen to us, but it does mean He will be there for us. He will help us through whatever is going on in our lives. We can call on Him, ask Him for help, because He does care and He will be there when we call. We should not fear, tremble, or worry because He tells us not to. Trust Him today with every concern, every problem, every heartache. He is on our side. He is our defender.

Prayer: Oh Lord, thank You that I can call out to You to save me, to help me, and to be my defense. I trust in You today. Amen.

Prayers, Thoughts, Gifts of Joy Today:

JULY 26

"When you pass through the waters, I will be with you; and through the rivers, they will not overcome you: when you walk through the fire, you will not be burned. . . ."

-ISAIAH 43:2

I read this verse the week after my mother's funeral, and it helped give me strength. My feelings of grief and sadness seemed to be flooding over me, swallowing me up. This verse and God's promise to be with me helped lift me up. It is important to read God's Word at all times, but especially when we are burdened and low. His Words will comfort and help us in times of distress. His Word will sustain us when everything around us is falling apart. There are times in our lives when we just don't see how we are going to make it through, but God will help if we will call out to Him. He promises to be with us when we go through the waters of despair. He says they will not overcome you. When we go through the fires of trials, problems, heartache, loss, and tribulations, He will not let us be burned.

Prayer: Lord, thank You for keeping me through the bad times in life, for not letting these overwhelm or overtake me. Help me to look to You for my help and strength. Amen.

Prayers, Thoughts, Gifts of Joy Today:

JULY 27

"Let us therefore come boldly unto the throne of grace, that we may obtain mercy, and find grace to help in time of need."

-HEBREWS 4:16

We can go to God boldly in prayer because He has made a way for us to do this. He is our Heavenly Father, and we can go to Him and ask for help any time. Mercy means leniency, compassion, and forgiveness. Grace is the free and undeserved favor of God. We did nothing to deserve God's favor, forgiveness, or help, but Jesus Christ paid our debt for us, and through Him, we are given direct access to God. This is a marvelous gift to us as human beings. Prayer is a gift. We should use it daily.

Prayer: Thank You, God, for Your mercy and grace. Thank You for giving me the gift of prayer, that I can come boldly to You, my Creator and God. I need Your help today. Amen.

Prayers, Thoughts, Gifts of Joy Today:

". . . the righteous doth sing and rejoice."
-PROVERBS 29:6

When we are freed from guilt by Jesus Christ, we can sing and rejoice, be happy because of what He has done for us. He has made us righteous (good, free from guilt and sin). Every day that we live, we are blessed! Think on this and rejoice, be grateful and sing—or at least hum! We should be the happiest of all people because we have been made right because of our belief and faith in God. Sing and rejoice. Be happy today!

Prayer: Lord, I praise You. I rejoice and lift my voice to You today. Thank You for what You have done for me. Amen.

Prayers, Thoughts, Gifts of Joy Today:

JULY 29

> "... trust—in the living God, who giveth us richly all things to enjoy."
>
> -1 TIMOTHY 6:17

We should put our trust in God, not in anything or anyone else, because He will give us the best—the things mere money cannot buy. He gives everlasting life, true inner peace, joy, love, forgiveness, heart happiness, contentment, and fulfillment. We are His children, and He wants to bless us with right things in our life. Trust Him today. He has given us "ALL" things to enjoy. He created this beautiful world, the flowers, trees, rivers, the animals, all of nature. He created joy and laughter. Think about this. He gives it all to us, His children, to enjoy. What a wonderful God we serve.

Prayer: Lord, I do trust You. Help me to trust You even more throughout this day and every day of my life. Help me to enjoy all You have given me. Thank You. Amen.

Prayers, Thoughts, Gifts of Joy Today:

JULY 30

"For the Lord God will help me. . . ."

-ISAIAH **50:7**

The Lord God is there for us and will help us. This is a powerful verse. It should give us comfort and encouragement. We can go to God with every need and He will help. We should never be disheartened when we really think about this. He will help. He is there with us through every day of our life—ready to help. This verse simply states, "The Lord God will help me." What a promise! Read it and memorize the verse to recall when we need reminding that He is there for us.

Prayer: Lord, thank You for being here with me and helping me with every area of my life. I can count on You. I sometimes feel distressed and down, but You lift me up again. Thank You. Amen.

Prayers, Thoughts, Gifts of Joy Today:

JULY 31

**"Do all things without murmurings and com-
plaining: that ye may be blameless and harm-
less, the sons of God, without rebuke. . . ."**
                                      -PHILIPPIANS 2:14-15

D o everything readily and cheerfully—no bickering, no
fussing allowed! Go out into the world uncorrupted;
be a breath of fresh air in this squalid and polluted society.
Provide people with a glimpse of good living and of the living God. We can be different in the world by being who God
wants us to be. It is difficult not to murmur or complain. I
catch myself doing this all the time. It is in our nature to complain and fuss, but we have to watch ourselves and work to
overcome this habit, because it is a habit. When we are aware
of this, we can do more to stop this thinking, this murmur-
ing, and complaining. Make a pact with me today to try and
watch it, stop it, and restructure our thoughts and words to
go to a higher place.

Prayer: God, help me to be the person You would have me
be in my world today. When I start to fuss or complain,
bring it to my attention so that I can stop immediately, and
then help me to say only kind, good, helpful words. Help
me have a better attitude. Thank You. With Your strength,
I can. Amen.

Prayers, Thoughts, Gifts of Joy Today:

AUGUST 1

". . . not by might, nor by power, but by my spirit, saith the Lord of hosts."

-ZECHARIAH 4:6

We can do nothing on our own that is of lasting good without the Lord's might, power, and spirit. When we try to do it alone, we will fail and fall, but with God's Spirit helping us, we will succeed! We can ask for His Spirit, His might, His power in our life today. Give Him all the glory for what He has done through us. We can conquer our fears, our doubts, our weaknesses, our sins, and our problems with His Spirit and His help. All things are possible for us when we look to Jesus to help us. We are nothing alone, but with God, we are unstoppable.

Prayer: God, help me today. Give me Your Spirit, Your might, and Your power every step of my way. I give You the glory for everything. Thank You. Amen.

Prayers, Thoughts, Gifts of Joy Today:

"Glory and honor are in his presence; strength and gladness are in his place."

-1 CHRONICLES 16:27

Glory, honor, strength, gladness. These are all wonderful words—words we want to have said to describe us. When we stay in the presence of God, in His place, near to His heart, then we can have these attributes. He will give them to our lives. Strive today to become what He wants us to be, to give glory and honor to Him as we live our lives. Daily living in the strength of the Lord is easier than going it alone. When we begin our day asking for His strength and His help, our day will run smoother, our attitude will be better, and our working relationships will be more peaceful because we will treat people as we would like to be treated. We won't lose our temper quite as easily. We will think before we speak. We will try to use wisdom in dealing with others. Oh, we won't be perfect, but we will be in a much better place.

Prayer: Bless me, Lord, with glory, honor, strength, and gladness, I pray. Help me today to treat others as I would want to be treated, to think of others, to care and show I care. Let me be a better person. Thank You. Amen.

Prayers, Thoughts, Gifts of Joy Today:

AUGUST 3

"Sing unto the Lord, all the earth. . . ."

-1 CHRONICLES 16:23

Sing! Make melody in our heart to the Lord. Praise His holy name. Lift our praises to the Lord today. Listening to great music blesses me, and when I think that God created music for us to enjoy, I am excited. He put a song in our hearts. Do you catch yourself singing or humming sometimes? God gave us this melody in our very hearts. Thank Him today. Smile and sing!

Think about it. God gave us music, some the ability to sing, to speak, some to play instruments, the ability to laugh, to dance, and to hear singing and laughter. What gifts these are. I know that due to disabilities, some people aren't able to do all of these things. But in our world, many disabilities have been overcome, so there are other ways to enjoy some of these things. We should be thankful for what we can enjoy because of God's gifts to us.

Prayer: Thank You, Lord, for music, for songs. I am blessed because of this. I praise You today. Let me sing or make melody in my heart to You today, Lord. Amen.

Prayers, Thoughts, Gifts of Joy Today:

AUGUST 4

**"For great is the Lord, and greatly to be praised:
he also is to be feared above all gods."**

-1 Chronicles 16:25

Our God, the true living God, is great, and the only true God. All other lowercase gods cannot and will not defeat Him. We are to hold Him in reverence and esteem, praise and worship Him, and honor Him by our words and deeds. When we forget just who He is, we are in trouble. Think today anew about the Lord God and His true greatness. We should be more afraid of hurting Him than being so cautious of other people's thinking about us. Stand strong for the Lord. Bless and praise Him. Be bold for our Lord today.

Prayer: Lord, help me to be strong in my convictions and in my life for You. Never let me shame You by my words or deeds. Thank You for helping me to be strong. Amen.

Prayers, Thoughts, Gifts of Joy Today:

AUGUST 5

"Let the heavens be glad, and let the earth rejoice: and let me say among the nations, the Lord reigneth."

-1 CHRONICLES 16:31

The Lord reigns over the world and is in control. We may not like what's happening in our world and things may seem out of control to us, but we can take peace and have confidence because the Bible tells us He is in control, and we have read the ending. Let us rejoice and be happy as we go through this day. Let the joy of the Lord sustain us and lift us up, knowing He is there through every situation. No matter what is happening in our life, He is there. He knows and understands how we feel. He reigns. When we hear too much bad news, we might want to open God's Word and read His news to overcome our fear. We are to rejoice and be glad because God is in control!

Prayer: Lord, I will rejoice and be joyful today because You reign in my life. When there may be problems all around me, You are my hope and my foundation. You are in control. Thank You. Amen.

Prayers, Thoughts, Gifts of Joy Today:

"O give thanks unto the Lord; for he is good; for his mercy endureth forever."

-1 CHRONICLES **16:34**

Give thanks always to God, for He is good to us. Because of his mercy, we are not consumed. He forgives, loves us, and keeps us daily. He will be with us forever and ever! We are so blessed. Let us think on this and remember this every day of our life. Because of our Lord, we live, breathe, laugh, love, and have joy. And even through difficult times, He is there with us, holding our hand and carrying us through. Oh, give thanks! There are times in our life when we have a pity party for ourselves. At these times, we have to remember He is good to us and His mercy goes on forever. We should never give up and give in to doubts and fears when things are going wrong for us. Hang on. He will get us through.

Prayer: Lord, I do thank You for ALL You have done for me. Thank You for Your love and mercy. Amen.

Prayers, Thoughts, Gifts of Joy Today:

AUGUST 7

**"Humble yourselves therefore under the mighty
hand of God, that he may exalt you in due time."**
-1 PETER 5:6

Humble is translated to mean "respectful, submissive,
modest, not proud or boastful, not thinking of yourself
as better than other people, not arrogant." -Webster

I especially liked the definition out of the Urban Dictionary:
"An admirable quality that not many people possess. It means
that a person may have accomplished a lot, or be a lot, but doesn't
feel it is necessary to advertise or brag about it."

God tells us to be humble, to submit to Him, and let His
hand lead and guide us. We can't do that if we feel we know as
much as God. We should strive to be humble in God's sight.

Prayer: I submit myself to Your Will today, Lord. Guide me,
please, I pray. Thank You. Amen.

Prayers, Thoughts, Gifts of Joy Today:

"For I have satiated the weary soul, and I have replenished every sorrowful soul."

                                                                -JEREMIAH 31:25

" For I have (satisfied) the weary soul—filled to overflowing—and replenished (renewed, refreshed, restored) every sorrow-filled soul." Sandra Wright's translation of this verse. If we ask God, He will satisfy and restore us. He is there for us every day, through every problem, sorrow, or fear. We often get mad at Him because we may feel He has allowed this trouble, this sorrow, this trial to come upon us. We know that He could have kept "this" from happening. Well, yes, He could have, but He didn't. If we believe in Him and trust Him, we know there was a reason for "this" in our lives. We must pray for Him to help us through "this," and if there is something for us to learn, that we learn it. We can grow to be a stronger Christian, a better person. There may be some way we can help another who is hurting because of what we have been through ourselves.

Prayer: Thank You, God, for filling me, for helping me through this sorrow, this pain, this problem. Let me learn more about You and Your will for me through this. Help me to deal with "this" and keep on keeping on. I trust You. Amen.

Prayers, Thoughts, Gifts of Joy Today:

AUGUST 9

> "He only is my rock and my salvation: he is my defense; I shall not be moved. In God is my salvation and my glory: the rock of my strength, and my refuge is in God. Trust in him at all times . . . pour out your heart before him. God is a refuge for us."
>
> -PSALM 62:6-8

God is our rock, a steady and firm foundation. He is strength and security and the one to run to when troubled. He is a strong and mighty fortress and our defense. We can stand strong because He is on our side; we can put our trust in Him and put our lives in His hands. This verse is a great one to memorize and quote aloud when we are feeling weak and helpless. This verse will make us stronger. Read it over again; speak it aloud to yourself. Find comfort and help in this verse.

Prayer: Thank You, God, for this verse of strength. Give me Your help and extra strength today as I face _____. Thank You. Amen.

Prayers, Thoughts, Gifts of Joy Today:

AUGUST 10

"For he satisfieth the longing soul, and filleth the hungry soul with goodness."

-Psalm 107:9

J esus satisfies our soul. He quenches the hunger and thirst of our hearts and fills us up with all good things. When we are down and discouraged, lonely and scared, we can turn to Him, for He alone can satisfy our souls. He will fill us up with joy unstoppable. He can and He will. Ask Him today. We may have thought that things, money, power, position, etc. will satisfy us, but we quickly find out these will not last. For lasting satisfaction and security, turn to Jesus. He satisfies the longing soul.

Prayer: Satisfy my soul today, Lord Jesus. Fill me with Your joy, and I will praise Your name. Thank You. Amen.

Prayers, Thoughts, Gifts of Joy Today:

AUGUST 11

". . . I am with you always, even unto the end of the world."

-MARK 28:20

J esus is with us every day of our lives. He is there for us through every situation. He will go with us until the end of this world, and then He promises He has prepared a place for us in heaven. What a wonderful blessing these promises are to us. We can count on Him to hold us up. Trust Him. When life gets bumpy and rough, He is with us, even to the end of our world. Think about this. There is great hope in this verse, telling us that God is with us always, for all the days of our life.

Prayer: Jesus, thank You for being with me today through every situation. Help me. Amen.

Prayers, Thoughts, Gifts of Joy Today:

AUGUST 12

"Those things, which ye have both learned, and received, and heard, and seen in me, do: and the God of peace shall be with you."

-PHILIPPIANS 4:9

I f we will read the Bible, we will learn, receive, and hear the principles, the teachings of Christ. Then, if we will apply these to our life, we will have peace inside. God's Word is a source of love and peace for us every day. His Word is strong and powerful, yet sweet and calming at the same time. This is a mystery, but so true. Only God can give us real inner peace. His presence gives us the strength to face every day with confidence and peace. The world around us causes us worry and stress, but when we are reading God's Word and praying for His help, we can face it all because He is there with us, helping us. When we learn, hear, and receive His promises to us, we can find His gentle peace so we can get through anything the world throws at us.

Prayer: Lord, let me learn, receive, hear, and do Your will today. Lead me through Your Word. Let me apply Your principles to my everyday life and live for You. I want Your peace. Thank You. Amen.

Prayers, Thoughts, Gifts of Joy Today:

AUGUST 13

"Set a watch, O Lord, before my mouth; keep the door of my lips."

-PSALM 140:3

We should pray this verse for God to help us watch our words. Try to allow only good words to come from our mouths—words that will build up, help, comfort, cheer, encourage, and show love. If we ask the Lord to help us, He will do so. This would be a great verse to pray every morning before getting out of bed. "Lord, guard my mouth." If we have children, grandchildren, family who live with us, this is a good verse to pray with them each day. All of us need to keep a watch on our words, don't we? Words have great power: to hurt, to tear down, or, on the other hand, to bless, to build up, and to encourage others. Let us commit to using our words, our lips, today to bless, to heal, to encourage, and to help those whom God puts in our life.

Prayer: Lord, help me to stay aware of my words, to speak only kind, good words today. Guard my mouth and my heart. Thank You. Amen.

Prayers, Thoughts, Gifts of Joy Today:

AUGUST 14

"Thou shalt make me full of joy with thy countenance."

-ACTS **2:28**

When Jesus looks upon us with His love, we can be filled with joy! His love and care are such a true blessing. We, His children, are never alone. When we know this—and accept this—it will fill us with joy, with such peace and comfort, that we will have extra strength and confidence in our lives, knowing we are never alone. God Himself is there with us, to fill us with joy. This is another verse that tells us having joy in the Lord is a good thing. God wants His children to be joyful and happy. The Bible tells us this over and over. When we have God Almighty as our Heavenly Father, why should we not be joyful?

Prayer: Thank You, God, for giving me Your joy today. Let me share it with others whom I meet today, my family, and friends. Amen.

Prayers, Thoughts, Gifts of Joy Today:

AUGUST 15

**". . . overflow with hope by the power of the
Holy Spirit."**

-**ROMANS 15:13**

Hope—what a wonderful blessing! God gives us hope when we trust in Him. He gives us hope for today, for tomorrow, and for our eternity. We are blessed. We should keep moving forward and look up always with hope. Hope is what makes our lives livable. Without hope, we would wither up and die. We would have a sad and miserable life. God gives us hope. Hope is one of my favorite words. It is a word of encouragement, a word full of life, full of joy. This verse says to "overflow with hope," and we can only "overflow" by the power of the Holy Spirit.

Prayer: Lord, thank You for the gift of hope. My hope is in You. Amen.

Prayers, Thoughts, Gifts of Joy Today:

August 16

". . . thou dost make me hope."

G od puts hope inside us. He fills us with hope, a gift of encouragement. Because of Jesus, we have this hope.

"With Jesus you do not have a hopeless end but an endless hope."

This quote is powerful. Read it again and think on what it says. We, as Christians, can face anything the world throws at us because we have hope through Jesus Christ. We may be going through a problem, a heartache, a hurt, but Jesus will give us strength and hope and carry us through. Praise His name today.

Prayer: Thank You, Jesus, for this endless hope, Your strength, and power! Amen.

Prayers, Thoughts, Gifts of Joy Today:

AUGUST 17

"I know that thou canst do everything. . . ."
                                        -JOB 42:2

We must remind ourselves often that God can do anything and everything. He is an all-powerful, all-knowing God. It is He who created us. He loves us and cares for us. So why then do we worry and fret? Because we lose sight of who He really is. This is one of the main reasons we should read our Bible, pray, study, and meditate on His Word. The Bible is His love letter and guidebook to us. Read it today. Recharge with faith and trust in God, knowing He can do anything and everything!

Prayer: Lord, I know You can do anything. Help me to follow You more and not depend on myself rather than You. Thank You for Your Word. Amen.

Prayers, Thoughts, Gifts of Joy Today:

AUGUST 18

"For by grace are ye saved through faith; and that not of yourselves: it is the gift of God: not of works, lest any man should boast. For we are his workmanship, created in Christ Jesus unto good works, which God hath before ordained that we should walk in them."

-EPHESIANS 2:8-10

G race is the free and undeserved favor of God. We don't do anything to deserve His salvation, but He asks us to have faith (complete trust or confidence) in Him. Works do not earn us salvation, although we are created to do as Christ and do good works on this earth. We should want to do good works when we accept Jesus Christ as our Savior. If our hearts are right with Him, we will want to do good works. Good works alone do not save us. Our salvation is given as a gift of God through grace and faith.

Prayer: Lord Jesus, thank You for the gift of salvation. Guide me to see where good works are needed and to use my gifts and talents to do good works for Your honor and glory. Give me the willingness and strength to do good works in Your name. Amen.

Prayers, Thoughts, Gifts of Joy Today:

AUGUST 19

". . . call upon me, and ye shall go and pray unto me, and I will hearken unto you."

-JEREMIAH 29:12

In the Bible, God exhorts us to call on Him, to pray, to ask Him. He promises to hear and listen to us. His answer may not always be what we want it to be, but He does hear and answer. He knows what we need and when we need the answer. We must trust Him because He knows best for our life. He knows the whole picture, not just the small view we see. We can and should trust Him, call out to Him, ask Him, and then expect His answer. Hold on to His promises, His Word from the Bible. Often, we just don't understand why things are happening as they do in our life or in the life of others. Our understanding is limited by our knowledge of God and His ways. He sees the future, our eternity, all that is ahead, and He knows in ways we do not. We must trust Him, and when we pray, ask "if it be Your will, Lord."

Prayer: Lord, thank You for the ability to pray, for allowing us to come to You. Thank You for hearing our prayers. Your will be done! Amen.

Prayers, Thoughts, Gifts of Joy Today:

AUGUST 20

**"Mine eyes are unto thee, O God the Lord: in
thee is my trust; leave not my soul destitute."**
-PSALM 141:8

Trust in the Lord God. Keep our eyes focused on Him
and His truths. This will keep us on a steady course in
life. His Word says He will neither leave nor forsake us. Hold
on to that promise, even when we go through trials and difficulties. He is there, even in our darkest hours. His Word
gives us many promises on which to stand firm. Read these.
We should write them on our hearts. Memorize the Words of
God. The Bible tells us over and over again to trust Him and
look to Him. We can trust Him with our life today. He will
not leave our souls destitute. He will restore our souls.

Prayer: O God, I put my trust in You today. I look to You
for strength and help each day. Thank You for always
being there and never leaving me. Amen.

Prayers, Thoughts, Gifts of Joy Today:

AUGUST 21

"I give unto them eternal life; and they shall never perish, neither shall any man pluck them out of my hand."

-JOHN 10:28

"My Father, which gave them me, is greater than all; and no man is able to pluck them out of my Father's hand. I and my Father are one."

-JOHN 10:29

We are promised here by Jesus' own words that when we trust Him and He is our shepherd, we have eternal life and will never perish, and no one can take us from His hand. He holds us and will not let us go. These are powerful verses—verses that should give us great comfort and security. We have everlasting life through Jesus Christ. We will never perish. No man can take this from us. No matter what others can do to us, Jesus has us in His hand. We can and should stand firm and secure in this knowledge.

Prayer: Thank You, Lord, for salvation, eternal life, and security because You will never let me go. I am held in Your hand. Amen.

Prayers, Thoughts, Gifts of Joy Today:

"Gracious is the Lord . . . the Lord saves . . . I was brought low and he helped me. For thou hast delivered my soul from death, mine eyes from tears, and my feet from falling."

-PSALM 116:5-8

The Lord our God protects, saves, and preserves us. He is gracious and merciful. When we are brought low, sad, brokenhearted by life, He is there to keep us from falling. He lifts us up and sets our feet on solid ground. He holds our hand and will never let us go. This is great news for us! Know that He is always with us, through every trial, through every day. Keep on praising. Keep on keeping on! He will deliver us.

Prayer: Lord, keep close to me through this day and keep me strong in the light of Your presence and protection. Thank You. Amen.

Prayers, Thoughts, Gifts of Joy Today:

AUGUST 23

"Continue in prayer; and watch in the same with thanksgiving."

-**COLOSSIANS 4:2**

Always give thanks and be thankful in all things. Pray and expect great things. God loves us and wants to bless us and give us good. When we are thankful and grateful, we are blessed even more because we notice and see the gifts God has given us. Look for God's gifts in our lives every day. Watch for them; expect wonderful things. Write a list of everything for which we are thankful today. I find when I am down and low, I can start writing my list of blessings and my spirits will rise. This has a therapeutic effect. When we pray and are thankful, we receive blessings in our hearts just from having prayed.

"Focus on the good life—and be thankful for it."

-**HAL URBAN**

Prayer: Thank You, God, for the wonderful gift of this new day. I am grateful for the sunrise this morning. Let me shine for You today. Amen.

Prayers, Thoughts, Gifts of Joy Today:

AUGUST 24

"Let your speech be always with grace, seasoned with salt, that ye may know how ye ought to answer every man."

-COLOSSIANS 4:6

Speak graciously, elegantly, and with kindness, but with preserving God's teachings in mind. Watch our words and deeds carefully. Pay close attention to what we say, not being careless or unthoughtful. Keep close to the Lord and ask Him to guard our heart and mouth throughout our day, so that we may bring Him honor and glory always. Our lives are meant to bring Him glory and honor; our words are meant to heal and help others.

"Kind words can be short and easy to speak, but their echoes are truly endless."

-MOTHER TERESA

Prayer: Lord, guard my heart and my words that they may be pleasing to You today. Thank You. Amen.

Prayers, Thoughts, Gifts of Joy Today:

> **"Now the God of peace . . . make you perfect in every good work to do his will, working in you that which is well pleasing in his sight, through Jesus Christ; to whom be glory forever and ever. Amen."**
>
> **-HEBREWS 13:20-21**

The above verse is a prayer of blessing for us—for us to do good work and be in God's will. We want to be well-pleasing in His eyes and to give Jesus Christ the glory always. Amen and Amen.

We know we will never be "perfect," but with God's help, we can work toward being more like Christ. We can work toward being pleasing to Him by the way we live, talk, and do. Striving to please God with our lives is a great goal, one we should all have. When we achieve this goal, we will be successful.

> **"My goal is to make life less difficult and more joyful for those around me."**
>
> **-SANDRA MANSFIELD WRIGHT**

Prayer: Oh Lord, let me be pleasing to You. Let me do Your will, and bring glory to You today in everything I do or say. Thank You. Amen.

Prayers, Thoughts, Gifts of Joy Today:

"I am with thee, and will keep thee in all places whither thou goest. . . ."

-GENESIS 28:15

God is with us and will continue to be with us wherever we go. He is there in every situation—good or bad. Know this. Be aware of this and seek His face. Even when bad things are happening, we can trust God to keep us and help us get through this time. Our heart may be broken into with grief and pain; know He is there with us. He knows and will help. Pain is part of life. Weeping may last for the night, but He will give us joy again! The Bible promises this to us. Trust Him. Have hope!

"Go into the sunshine and be happy with what you see."

-WINSTON CHURCHILL

Prayer: Oh Lord, help me through this pain. Help me to find my joy again. Lift me up. Help me to stand firm on You. Thank You. Amen.

Prayers, Thoughts, Gifts of Joy Today:

AUGUST 27

"Give unto the Lord the glory due unto his name. . . ."

-PSALM 29:2

What is the Lord due from us? Everything we are. All we have. He is due glory, worship, honor, and our very lives. He created us, and we are His. When we stop and think about who God is and what He has done for us, we should never be flippant and nonchalant about Him in any way. He demands and deserves our respect and honor always. How do we respect and honor Him? By living our lives in such a way that is pleasing to Him. We do this by praying and reading His Word and living by the principles of His Word.

Prayer: God, I praise and worship You today because of who You are; my Savior and Redeemer. Help me to live my life in such a way that will be pleasing and bring honor to You. Thank You. Amen.

Prayers, Thoughts, Gifts of Joy Today:

AUGUST 28

"Casting down imaginations, and every high thing that exalteth itself against the knowledge of God, and bringing into captivity every thought to the obedience of Christ."

-2 CORINTHIANS 10:5

We should bring our thoughts under the control of Jesus Christ by prayer and the study of His Word. The study of His Word, His teachings, and His principles helps us to stand strong against the false knowledge the world often sends out. We, as Christians, must know God's Word and be aware of His teachings so we do not fall under the spell of false doctrine and teachings. It is so easy to follow charismatic people. They talk, we listen, and easily fall into their teachings without checking out the Word of God for ourselves. We should be careful not to just follow blindly, but to consider the words carefully, watch actions to see if they match with God's teachings, and be on guard. "When my eyes can't see and my mind cannot comprehend, still my heart will trust." I wrote this several years ago and still believe it today.

Prayer: God, give me Your wisdom and knowledge, and help me to know the difference between right and wrong in the world. When the world confuses me, keep me coming back to Your teachings. Thank You. Amen.

Prayers, Thoughts, Gifts of Joy Today:

"Now unto him that is able to keep you from falling, and to present you faultless before the presence of his glory with exceeding joy, to the only wise God our Savior, be glory and majesty, dominion and power, both now and ever. Amen."

Only God can keep us and give us true joy! We can trust Him with our today and our forevermore. He is the only wise God, our Savior. Give Him the glory with our life this very day. Ask Him to help us, to keep us from falling, to hold us up, protect, and guide us. Thank Him. Joy only comes through Jesus Christ. He created joy. He wants us to have joy, "exceeding joy." To have joy in our lives, we must be aware of all the wonderful things God is giving us, to reach out for them, to accept them. We miss much joy because we aren't watching for it. Watch for it today.

"Simply be aware of the wonderful things that are happening in your life."

-NORMAN VINCENT PEALE

Prayer: Lord God, my Savior and Redeemer, thank You for always being here with me. Keep my feet from stumbling and me from falling. Keep me close to You. Let me see and take joy. Thank You. Amen.

Prayers, Thoughts, Gifts of Joy Today:

"Christ in you, the hope of glory."

-COLOSSIANS **1:27**

When we accept Christ and invite Him into our heart, our life, He then sends us His Holy Spirit to be in us. He then seals us as His own and gives us the promise, the hope of glory. We are His forever, and nothing can separate us from Him and His love—nothing!!! This is amazing and so wonderful! Because Christ lives in us, we can have hope!

"Defeat need not be the end result."

-GLENN VAN EKEREN

Prayer: Thank You, Jesus, for being my hope, my strength, my Savior, my everything! Amen.

Prayers, Thoughts, Gifts of Joy Today:

AUGUST 31

> "I the Lord have called thee in righteousness, and will hold thine hand, and will keep thee . . . ."
>
> -ISAIAH 42:6

The Lord will hold our hand and keep us so that nothing can snatch us away. We are secure in His hand. There is no need to worry, fret, be upset, or anxious about anything. We can trust Him completely. Read His Word and remain strong. The more we read the Bible and pray, the stronger and more at peace we will become. His promises are all through the Bible— promises like the above verse. Thank Him and trust Him. When we are struggling with life, go to the life-giver. He is holding our hand right now. He won't let go. Don't worry. Trust Him now.

> "Even the darkest night will end and the sun will rise."
>
> -VICTOR HUGO

Prayer: Lord, let me know You are holding my hand. I thank You in everything today. Help me to trust You even more. Take this dark night from my life if it be Your will, and give me Your joy and light. Amen.

Prayers, Thoughts, Gifts of Joy Today:

SEPTEMBER 1

". . . because his compassions fail not. They are new every morning: great is thy faithfulness."
-LAMENTATIONS 3:22-23

The Lord has compassion on us. Every morning, we are blessed by His mercy and grace. We should be thankful and filled with praise every new day. He is faithful and true to us. All of His promises He will keep. People sometimes fail or disappoint us, but Jesus Christ will not fail us. He is faithful to us. I think of compassion as a loving look and thought toward us. He wants the best for us. He knows our frailties, yet accepts us anyway. He knows our thoughts, our motives, our sins, and yet loves us in spite of all of these. He wants to give us joy every day of our lives.

"Write it on your heart that every day is the best day of the year."
-EMERSON

Prayer: I praise You, Lord, for Your mercy, grace, compassion, and love. Thank You for this new day. Thank You for Your faithfulness to me. Amen.

Prayers, Thoughts, Gifts of Joy Today:

SEPTEMBER 2

"The Lord is my portion, saith my soul, therefore will I hope in him."

-LAMENTATIONS 3:24

Hope. Always hope because of the Lord! He is our salvation and our hope, our help in times of trouble. Hope is a wonderful blessing we are given as Christians. We have hope above all others because of our Lord and Savior, Jesus Christ. The Bible teaches hope. When we may feel we have no more hope, pray and hold on to the promises of God. He will give us joy and hope again. When the Lord is our portion—all we need in this life—then we have hope in Him. Pray today, and ask the Lord to put hope in our hearts again. Ask for renewed faith and hope. Hope in Him!

"Paint the walls of your mind with many beautiful pictures."

-WILLIAM LYON PHELPS

Prayer: Lord, my hope is in You, and I have hope because of You. Thank You for giving me the gift of hope. Amen.

Prayers, Thoughts, Gifts of Joy Today:

September 3

**"The Lord is good unto them that wait for him,
to the soul that seeketh him."**

-Lamentations 3:25

S eek the Lord, and you will find Him. He is good to us. He loves us and is here with us right now. We may not see Him in a bodily form, but with our hearts, we can trust Him. Think back over your life and remember all He has done for you, what He has brought you through up to this time. Hasn't He always been there for you? He will not forsake His children. We may go through hurts and troubles, but He is there with us through these. Because of Him, we can come through, knowing His strength will get us through. Don't give up. Don't give in. Keep on keeping on with the Lord by your side. He has you by your hand today.

Prayer: Thank You, Lord, for Your presence, Your love, Your care. Help me to wait for You and trust You more. Hold on tight to my hand. Amen.

Prayers, Thoughts, Gifts of Joy Today:

SEPTEMBER 4

"... let us offer the sacrifice of praise to God continually, that is, the fruit of our lips giving thanks to his name."

-HEBREWS 13:15

We should constantly be in a state of praise and thankfulness to God for all He has done, for His mercies and His goodness. His name should be glorified, lifted up, and given honor and glory. Think of what He has done for us. Praise His name forevermore! A sacrifice is something we offer up to God as a gift to Him, to honor and worship Him. We give Him our praise as a sign that we love Him. Praise Him today as a sacrifice of love. Praise. Be thankful! By doing this, we make our own day brighter.

"You make a difference in how your day and life work out."

-GLENN VAN EKEREN

Prayer: Thank You, God, for Your mercies and grace to me. Thank You for my life. Even when things are bad, You can turn them into joy for me by staying with me through it all. Amen.

Prayers, Thoughts, Gifts of Joy Today:

September 5

"I will offer to thee the sacrifice of thanksgiving, and will call upon the name of the Lord."
-Psalm 116:17

Give thanks to God daily for all His wondrous works, and for everything He has given us. Every blessing we enjoy comes from God. We have nothing without Him. When we realize this, then we can truly thank Him. Go about in a state of thanksgiving. Notice and be thankful throughout this day. In this way, we will see even more blessings as they open up to us. Again, this verse talks about sacrifice; this time, it is thanksgiving rather than praise. When we praise, we are usually thankful. Saying grace at the table before a meal is a form of offering thanksgiving and praise to God. Make this a choice we practice daily, to say a prayer of thanks before a meal. It is a simple act that will add much to our lives.

Prayer: Lord, I call on Your name this morning with praise and thankfulness for ALL the mighty, wondrous things You have done. You are worthy of all my praise. Thank You. Amen.

Prayers, Thoughts, Gifts of Joy Today:

SEPTEMBER 6

**"And let the peace of God rule in your hearts . . .
and be ye thankful."**

-COLOSSIANS 3:15

P ray and ask God to put peace in our heart. He will give us peace, calm, and a quiet and gentle spirit if we ask. The Bible tells us time and time again to "be thankful." Look for things for which to be thankful. Go about your day in a spirit of thankfulness. God likes us to say "thank you" to Him and to others. Appreciate; always appreciate! It costs us nothing, yet it gives great dividends.

Prayer: God, give me a peace and a calm in my heart today. There are so many things I think I need to do today, and I get caught up in the busyness of life. Give me Your peace, Your spirit of love and calm in my heart. And let me always notice and appreciate. Thank You, Lord. Amen.

Prayers, Thoughts, Gifts of Joy Today:

> **"Enter into his gates with thanksgiving and into his courts with praise: be thankful unto him, and bless his name."**
>
> **-Psalm 100:4**

B e thankful; praise and bless His Holy name. He is the One God—our God. He deserves our constant praise and adoration in everything we do and in all we are. It is because of Him that we have our very life and breath. Think about this! Praise be to God. Thankfulness, praise, worship, and honor should be always in our hearts and on our tongues. We are coming into the season of Thanksgiving in the next month. Start getting ready now by being thankful and appreciative in our hearts.

Prayer: Thank You, God, for my life, for this new day, for the very air I breathe, for everything! I love, praise, and worship You. Amen.

Prayers, Thoughts, Gifts of Joy Today:

SEPTEMBER 8

"Oh that men would praise the Lord for his goodness, and for his wonderful works to the children of men."

-PSALM 107:21

The Lord is good to us and has done wonderful things for us. We need not forget these things always. Praise His name and thank Him every morning. Be thankful always. We show Him our thankfulness and praise when we do His will in our lives, when we follow His teachings and principles from the Bible: His Word. When we try to live our lives by following His teachings, this shows our devotion and adoration. We can't be perfect, but the Bible tells us to try to be perfect and follow Christ. When we pray and ask His blessings and help, He will honor our prayers and help us. With His help, we can do this thing called life!

Prayer: Lord, I thank You for every blessing, every goodness, every wonderful work You have done. Help me to live for You today. Guide me. Protect me. Keep me in Your care. Thank You. Amen.

Prayers, Thoughts, Gifts of Joy Today:

SEPTEMBER 9

"And thou shalt love the Lord thy God with all thine heart, and with all thy soul, and with all thy might."

-DEUTERONOMY 6:5

What does it mean to love God with all our heart, soul, and might? To love Him with our whole being, with all we are, with all we have. This is what the Bible tells us to do. This may seem hard to do, but we should try to do this. When we pray for God's help to love Him more, He will give us His help, and with God, "all things are possible." When we do what He tells us to do, we will be happier, more fulfilled, and have a better life. He wants this for us. He only tells us to do things that are good for us.

Prayer: Lord, help me to love You with all my heart, all my soul, and all my might. Thank You for being here to help me do this. What You tell me to do, You will help me do. Amen.

Prayers, Thoughts, Gifts of Joy Today:

SEPTEMBER 10

"I am Alpha and Omega, the beginning and the ending, saith the Lord, which is, and which was, and which is to come, the Almighty."
-REVELATION **1:8**

God is ultimately in control. We are not. When we forget this and start to worry and fret, we get all out of whack. Trust. Trust. And trust some more. He is, and was, and is to come again. He created us. He loves and cares for us. It is going to be all right! It is! He has everything under His control! Really! When we let the world take over our lives, we start to worry and become anxious. When we think on the Lord and who He truly is, we can relax and leave it all up to Him. He will give us peace and a calm that the world can't take away.

Prayer: Oh Lord, our Maker, Redeemer, our Salvation, You are God Almighty! I trust You. You have everything under control. I can relax and breathe. When I start to get all out of control, calm my heart. Let me think on You. Thank You. Amen.

Prayers, Thoughts, Gifts of Joy Today:

SEPTEMBER 11

"Abide in me, and I in you. As the branch cannot bear fruit of itself, except it abide in the vine, no more can ye, except ye abide in me."

-JOHN 15:4

Abide in God. Take time to study His Word, pray to Him, and wait for Him. Let Him help us become who He intends us to be. He created us. He knows us. We must learn to know Him and His plans for our life. Bearing fruit, producing good in this world, is His ultimate goal for us. Some of the fruits that the Bible tells us about in Galatians, Chapter 5 are, "Love, joy, peace, longsuffering, gentleness, goodness, faith, meekness, temperance." We should work to have these fruits in our life. With God's help, we can have these fruits of the spirit when we abide in God's Word and ask Him to help us. It is difficult to always have love, joy, peace, etc. The world—we ourselves—get in our own way. We may lose our temper, say something unloving, not have an attitude of joy, etc. We have to keep striving for these attributes, even when we fail. Keep going toward the goal.

Prayer: Lord, help me to abide in You today. Please work in my life, and bring forth the fruits of Your Spirit. Thank You. Amen.

Prayers, Thoughts, Gifts of Joy Today:

SEPTEMBER 12

"He shall not be afraid of evil tidings: his heart is fixed, trusting in the Lord."

-PSALM 112:7

We will not be afraid even when we hear evil things. Stand firm without doubts and fears. Do not become unsteady or undecided, but always know God is faithful in His promises to us. He has promised in His Word never to leave us or forsake us. His love for us is steadfast, true, firm, and a constant. Profess Him proudly and be strong. Stay strong! Keep our hearts fixed and steady, trusting in the Lord.

Prayer: Lord Jesus, help me to always hold fast and strong in my faith and belief in You in this world. Thank You for Your promises to help me. Amen.

Prayers, Thoughts, Gifts of Joy Today:

SEPTEMBER 13

". . . the inward man is renewed day by day."
-II CORINTHIANS 4:16

To be renewed, refreshed, regenerated, and restored, we need to go to God every morning in prayer and study His Word. His Word and knowledge of it will lift us, encourage, and give us a life that is complete. His standards and principles are those we can live by daily. We will walk stronger and be confident when we rely on Him. He is our Creator, our Savior, our Redeemer— the one who loves and cares for us and will be with us throughout this life. We can be recharged and renewed every morning, day by day!

Prayer: Lord, renew me this morning. "Restore unto me the joy of Thy salvation." The world may get me down, but You, Lord, will lift me up again. Thank You. Amen.

Prayers, Thoughts, Gifts of Joy Today:

"He giveth power to the faint, and to them that have no might he increaseth strength."
-ISAIAH 40:29

God gives us the power and strength to overcome any problem or situation we may be facing. Do not give up or become discouraged. Ask God for help, power, and extra strength. He will be with us right where we are. He will see us through this. We can trust Him always—with anything. We can be strong and overcome this because we have Almighty God beside us every step of the way.

". . . they shall run, and not be weary; and they shall walk, and not faint."
-ISAIAH 40:31

Prayer: Lord, I ask You for Your power and increased strength today to get through what I am facing. Thank You for hearing my prayer and answering. Amen.

Prayers, Thoughts, Gifts of Joy Today:

SEPTEMBER 15

"Bring ye all the tithes into the storehouse and see . . . if I will not open you the window of heaven, and pour you out a blessing, that there shall not be room enough to receive it."
-MALACHI 3:10

We are to give our tithes to the Lord. He promises to open the windows of heaven and pour out blessings on us when we obey Him. Give freely and out of love to the Lord. He loves us and wants to bless us. Blessings are defined in the dictionary as "God's favor and protection, approval, leading to happiness." Many think this verse means God will give us money or material things, but I feel it is more than this—His protection and care, which is much more precious.

Prayer: Thank You, God, for Your favor and protection over my life. I am blessed. Help me to give to You with a giving, willing heart. Amen.

Prayers, Thoughts, Gifts of Joy Today:

SEPTEMBER 16

"For this God is our God for ever and ever: he will be our guide even unto death."

-PSALM 48:14

When we have the Lord by us, there is no reason to be afraid, even of death. With Him, we can face anything. He is the guide within us. We can have confidence because of Him. Let us learn to depend and rely on His guidance. As Christians, we should never allow discouragement and fear to defeat us. We sometimes do, though, don't we? Yes. But read this verse of strength and encouragement and recommit to our faith in God. It will help us to renew our hope in Him. Remember, Jesus used scriptures to quote aloud to Satan in His wilderness experience when tempted by Satan. Bible verses can and will defeat the enemy.

Prayer: Lord, thank You for being my guide through this day. Help me to depend on You to help me through when I am afraid or have worries, even unto death. Amen.

Prayers, Thoughts, Gifts of Joy Today:

September 17

"With him is wisdom and strength, he hath counsel and understanding."

-Job 12:13

We may have problems and sometimes feel we have been harmed, but we can know that God shields us from harm and gives us strength and a song. We are helped by Him daily. Be aware of His protection and care. Sing and speak words of praise and love to Him. He delights in our thanksgiving and our praise. There will be times in life when we go through hard things that life itself gives us. These may be of our own making because of the choices we have made, or due to another's hurt to us, or just life itself. Bad things sometimes happen, even to God's children; just look at Job. This doesn't mean God has forsaken us or allowed this harm to come on us because He doesn't love us. We may not understand it all until we get to heaven. I don't claim to have all the answers to life's problems, but God does. We read the Bible—God's Word—and take the verses He gives us and believe and trust in Him always, even when things are looking dark and dreary. He will never leave us or forsake us. He promises. Hold on to His strength and let Him be our shield.

Prayer: Thank You, Lord, for Your love and Your protection. I can rely on You no matter what comes. I praise Your name and lift up my song of praise to You today. Amen.

Prayers, Thoughts, Gifts of Joy Today:

SEPTEMBER 18

"In the multitude of my thoughts within me thy comforts delight my soul."

-PSALM 94:19

The Lord can give real comfort to our soul. When we become down and discouraged, we can turn to God for help and comfort. He will lift our thoughts and bring us through this difficult time. Rest in His mercy and grace. Depend on Him, not on ourselves. He is in ultimate control. He has this for us. We can find comfort and delight by trusting in Jesus Christ today. Things don't always happen the way we would like; we don't always get our way in this world. God will give us comfort and delight our soul when we trust and rely on Him.

Prayer: Lord, comfort my soul today, right now. I need Your comfort every hour. Sometimes my mind and thoughts go to worry and fretting, but when I put my mind and thoughts on You, I am comforted. Thank You. Amen.

Prayers, Thoughts, Gifts of Joy Today:

SEPTEMBER 19

"Fear ye not, stand still, and see the salvation of the Lord."

-EXODUS 14:13

Stand still. Be still. Don't be afraid. For the Lord, our God, has us in His capable hands, in His care. I have read that "faith is stronger than fear." When we have faith in Jesus, our fears are put into proper perspective. When our eyes are on Jesus, we can face our fears because He is there with us, helping us. We don't have to go through this alone. He will see us through the trials and problems of our life when we ask for His help. He doesn't always answer in the way we want, but we must remember that He sees the entire picture and knows what we need and when we need it. Standing still is difficult sometimes, just waiting and letting God handle things and not plunging ahead ourselves. Often this is exactly what we need to do—stand still and wait. We must pray and ask for wisdom here because there are times when we need to do and times when we need to be still. God will show us the right way when we pray sincerely about the situation.

Prayer: Oh Lord, thank You for being with me today and every day. You calm my fears and give me strength. Help me to know when to do and when to wait on You. Amen.

Prayers, Thoughts, Gifts of Joy Today:

". . . thou shalt be steadfast, and shall not fear."
-JOB 11:15

Steadfast, steady on, staying the course that we are set on—
that is what God wants for us. We don't have to fear anything because God is with us through every problem and trial
we face. He will keep us steady and hold us up. Trust God,
even when things are hard. Keep on keeping on. We have to
trust God with every fiber of our being. He has our back.
We don't have to be afraid. If we die, we are going to heaven,
right? My daddy used to say, "I'm not afraid of dying, but I
am afraid of the dying process." I understand that. We don't
know exactly what to expect, what we may have to go through
and endure before we go to heaven. Our trust and faith has to
see us through, though. Jesus said He will be with us through
everything, no matter what. So we will believe Him in His
promise. We will not fear because we have Him on our side.

Prayer: Lord, thank You for holding me up and making me
steady, for sitting my feet on solid, unshaking ground. Give
me a spirit of courage and strength today. Thank You.
Amen.

Prayers, Thoughts, Gifts of Joy Today:

"Thou shalt be secure, because there is hope."
-Job 11:18

There is hope because of the God we love and serve. When everything around us seems to be caving in, know that our God is still there, holding our hand, lifting us up. We can feel secure because of who He is and because of His promise to <u>never</u> leave us or forsake us. We may have moments in our lives when we feel alone, but we can know deep within that we are never alone! Never! He promises to be with us.

Prayer: Thank You, God, for being here with me through this day and through my tomorrows as well. I am never alone because You are with me always. I do not have to fear. I can have hope and be secure because of this. Amen.

Prayers, Thoughts, Gifts of Joy Today:

September 22

> ". . . Jesus Christ: whom having not seen, ye love; in who, though now ye see him not, yet believing, ye rejoice with joy unspeakable and full of glory."
>
> **-1 Peter 1:7-8**

Believe, love, and trust. Then rejoice with unbelievable, radiant joy! Jesus Christ gives us this amazing "full of glory" kind of joy. We should dance, sing, jump, and clap our hands with joy because of the God we serve. We have not seen Him, but we feel His Spirit in our hearts and life, and that Spirit causes us to "rejoice with joy unspeakable." We should be, of all people, most joyful and happy because we serve a risen Savior.

Prayer: Thank You, Jesus, for Your joy unspeakable. I am amazed today by Your love for me. Amen.

Prayers, Thoughts, Gifts of Joy Today:

SEPTEMBER 23

"If ye keep my commandments, ye shall abide in my love; even as I have kept my Father's commandments, and abide in his love. These things have I spoken unto you, that my joy might remain in you, and that your joy might be full."

-JOHN 15:10-11

G od wants us to have joy, to be full of joy! In the words above, Jesus Himself tells us how to have joy, full joy. He says to keep His commandments and abide in His love, to remain close to Him. When we drift away from Him and take our eyes off Him, that is when our joy starts to drift away. Notice this and keep our eyes and hearts near Jesus and our joy fresh daily. Daily fresh joy is renewed every morning when we pray and praise God. Lift up our hearts and lives to Him today, and let us have full joy!

Prayer: Lord Jesus, let me keep my eyes and heart on You today. Give me Your full joy. Thank You. Amen.

Prayers, Thoughts, Gifts of Joy Today:

SEPTEMBER 24

". . . this is the victory that overcometh the world, even our faith."

-1 JOHN 5:4

Faith: trust, belief, confidence, conviction. Faith is the victory that will overcome worldly things. When we believe and put our trust in Jesus Christ to help us through each day ahead, we will overcome, get through. With faith, all things are possible. We can trust Him to help us through today with whatever problem we are facing. We can look to Him, pray, and ask, trusting His will for our life. He will bring us through. He may not take us out of the problem, but He will give us the strength to get through.

Prayer: Lord, help me today. Give me wisdom and strength. Lead and guide me in everything I do. Thank You. Amen.

Prayers, Thoughts, Gifts of Joy Today:

SEPTEMBER 25

". . . we should live soberly, righteously, and godly, in this present world; looking for that blessed hope, and the glorious appearing of the great God and our Savior Jesus Christ."

-TITUS **2:12-13**

Blessed hope. What is this blessed hope? As Christians, our hope is in and through Jesus Christ. This scripture encourages us to live the Christian life seriously, to take our beliefs strongly, and to live with a blessed hope. God gives us hope always. When our world seems to be caving in, problems seem to be pressing in on all sides, and worries are piling up over us, we can know we serve a great God and He is our Savior. He will help us. We can have a blessed hope that He will help us always. He will not forsake us.

Prayer: Lord, thank You for blessed hope! Let me keep on keeping on, hoping in You always. Amen.

Prayers, Thoughts, Gifts of Joy Today:

**"Therefore my heart is glad, and my glory rejoi-
ceth: my flesh also shall rest in hope."**

-PSALM 16:9

B e glad (happy), rejoice, and rest in hope. We have great
hope and expectations from God. The scriptures are
filled with hope and encouragement to us, His children. He
tells us over and over again that we are loved. He tells us He
has our hand and will not let us go, that He is there for us.
He promises to come again, and He tells us He has gone to
prepare a place for us where we will live eternally with Him.
We can rejoice, hope, and be glad!

Prayer: Thank You, God, for all Your promises of hope in
the Bible and for the blessing of hope. Amen.

Prayers, Thoughts, Gifts of Joy Today:

"I trusted in thee, O Lord: I said, thou art my God."

-PSALM 31:14

We need to trust Him because, otherwise, we will be struggling and miserable. Ultimately, God is the one in control, not us. Think on this. What good will worry, fighting against God, planning, and pushing for our way do? Let go. Trust. Obey. Go the way He wants. He created us. He has the best plan for our life. He gave us the personality, the talents, and the gifts we possess. He has a plan for our life. Listen to His gentle guidance. Trust in God. He is our God.

Prayer: Thank You, God, for Your gentle guidance in my life. Let me be wise enough to hear and follow You. Amen.

Prayers, Thoughts, Gifts of Joy Today:

SEPTEMBER 28

"For all the gods of the nations are idols: but the Lord made the heavens. Honour and majesty are before him: strength and beauty are in his sanctuary."

-PSALM 96:5-6

G ive the Lord honor and bow before him. He deserves our praise, our adoration, and in His very presence can be found strength and beauty. Every other god people worship: money, position, praise, power, possessions, family, or other philosophies or world gods are mere idols. See them as such, and set our minds and hearts on the one true God!

Prayer: Lord, I hope in You today. I give you honor and my worship. Strengthen my heart. Thank You. Amen.

Prayers, Thoughts, Gifts of Joy Today:

SEPTEMBER 29

"Thou art my hiding place; thou shalt preserve me from trouble; thou shalt compass me about with songs of deliverance."

-PSALM 32:7

The Lord is a place we can run to and find shelter and comfort from the troubles of the world. He will surround or encompass us with His arms of love and protection. We can find deliverance through Him. When we feel overwhelmed, unsettled, upset, or disturbed, we can run to Him and find His comfort and help. Remember, "There is nothing that you and God together can't handle." Nothing!

Prayer: Lord, thank You for being my safe place, my comforter, my shield, my shelter from the storms, my Redeemer, and my friend. I run to You and am safe. Amen.

Prayers, Thoughts, Gifts of Joy Today:

"Be of good cheer; it is I, be not afraid."
                                    -**MATTHEW 14:27**

We should be full of cheer because God Almighty is with us! We should not be afraid. We become afraid when we stop looking at Jesus and see the world around us—all our problems, worries, and difficulties. Jesus has everything we need to take away these things from our mind. Focus on Him. Look to Him for strength and courage today. Refocus our attention, our heart, and mind on Him, and things of this world will grow dim and come into true perspective.

Prayer: Lord, thank You for being here with me today, right now, where I am. Keep my eyes focused on You so that I can see things in a clear light. Amen.

Prayers, Thoughts, Gifts of Joy Today:

OCTOBER 1

"I will look unto the Lord; I will wait for the God of my salvation: my God will hear me."
-MICAH 7:7

Look to the Lord for help to live day to day. God hears us and knows our heart. He is there, always. Look to Him for our help every single day. Do not allow the doubts, fears, and troubles of this world to overcome us and discourage us. He is the God of help and salvation. Let Him lift us up today.

Prayer: Oh Lord, I look to You for my help and my salvation. I know You hear me and know my heart. Help me, I pray today. Thank You for always hearing me. Amen.

Prayers, Thoughts, Gifts of Joy Today:

OCTOBER 2

"When thou said, Seek ye my face; my heart said unto thee, thy face, Lord will I seek . . . thou hast been my help; leave me not, neither forsake me, O God of my salvation."

-PSALM 27:8-9

Seek His face. Read His Word. Pray, asking Him every day to help. He has promised in His Word to never leave us or forsake us. Trust His Word. Believe His Word, and know He has us in His hand. He is our Savior and our salvation. There are moments when we are hurting or going through grief or problems and we may cry out to God and even feel He has deserted us, but He has not. He is there and will be with us through this. Hang on to Him and His love. He will bring us through.

Prayer: Thank You, God, for never leaving me alone. Amen.

Prayers, Thoughts, Gifts of Joy Today:

"Why art thou cast down, O my soul? And why art thou disquieted within me? Hope in God: for I shall yet praise him, who is the health of my countenance, and my God."

-PSALM 43:5

E ven David, in the Bible, had moments of being down and worried. In this verse, he says, "Hope in God!" Don't lose hope. Don't give up. Be full of good courage. Keep on praising God because He is our health and life and our God. No matter what is happening around us, we can keep on praising and glorifying God. Doing this will lift our spirits.

"Crying cleanses the tear ducts, but laughter encourages the soul."

-GLENN VAN EKEREN

Prayer: Lord, I lift Your name up today. I praise You. My hope and strength are in You. Thank You always. Amen.

Prayers, Thoughts, Gifts of Joy Today:

"I will greatly rejoice in the Lord, my soul shall be joyful in my God."

-ISAIAH 61:10

Rejoice and be joyful because of what God has done for us. He has given us salvation, and He is with us always, even to the end of this world, and then throughout eternity. Focus our eyes on this; rejoice and be glad. We often take our eyes off God and start to focus on the world around us—its troubles and problems. Refocus, rethink, and find our joy in the Lord who has it all in His capable hands.

"Laughter is the most powerful state of mind there is. When you're laughing, you can't think of anything else."

-**H. JACKSON BROWN**

Laugh aloud today and praise God!

Prayer: Lord, help me to keep my eyes and thoughts on You today and to see who You are, who is really in charge of this world. Then I can let go of worry and just rejoice and laugh! Amen.

Prayers, Thoughts, Gifts of Joy Today:

OCTOBER 5

"The Lord is my rock, and my fortress, and my deliverer; my God, my strength, in whom I trust."

-PSALM 18:2

The Lord is our strong and firm foundation. In this world, when so many doctrines, different beliefs, and philosophies are all around us, it can get confusing. God is our foundation, our strength, our stronghold. Read His Holy Word and pray for wisdom and discernment. His principles, His Word, and His Spirit will lead you. When we truly pray and ask for His wisdom, He will lead.

Prayer: Lord, You are my rock, my fortress, my deliverance, my God, my strength, and my wisdom. I will not be afraid but will trust You. Thank You. Amen.

Prayers, Thoughts, Gifts of Joy Today:

OCTOBER 6

"For in thee, O Lord, do I hope: thou wilt hear, O Lord my God."

-PSALM 38:15

Our hope, our confidence is in the Lord. He hears us when we call on Him, and He will answer. He is our God and our help, our hope. We should not be fearful, worried, or bothered by all that is going on around us because God is here for us, to help, to lead, and to guide. Hope is a marvelous thing. When we trust in God and know His Word, we can feel secure in our hope and have great courage and strength to face whatever lies ahead of us. Now we don't need to be discouraged or beat ourselves up when we have doubts and fears; this is human. Even when we are walking close to the Lord, we can have times of doubt and fear. Just keep reading the Bible and praying. God will see us through. He promises to do this for us.

Prayer: Thank You, my God, for the blessing of hope today. When I start having doubts and fears, calm my soul, Lord, and give me Your peace and hope always. Amen.

Prayers, Thoughts, Gifts of Joy Today:

OCTOBER 7

"I will sing of thy power; yea, I will sing aloud of thy mercy in the morning: for thou hast been my defense and refuge in the day of my trouble."
-PSALM 59:16

We all have troubles. This is a universal truth. We may be in the very middle of a trouble, just coming out of one, or have those we love in the midst of a problem and are praying for them. In our days of trouble, we should remember always, God is there for us. He is our defense and our refuge. Run to Him and be safe. Remember playing hide and seek as a child? You would run to home base and be safe. God is our home base. He is our safety place. Run to Him today.

Prayer: Lord, thank You for never leaving or forsaking me in my day of trouble. I run to You and am safe. Amen.

Prayers, Thoughts, Gifts of Joy Today:

OCTOBER 8

"Unto thee, O my strength, will I sing; for God is my defense, and the God of my mercy."
-PSALM 59:17

He is our God, our defender, and has great mercy on us. Sing of His love to us. Praise His Holy name. Even if we feel we cannot sing, put on a song of praise and sing along. This act, in itself, will help us and lift up our spirit. God created music and gave humans the ability to hum and to sing, to make music in our hearts. He gave us music to enjoy. This was a wonderful gift. Praise Him with song and music. Recall songs that we knew as a child, possibly ones we learned in church. Write the words down and read them over again. This will bring to memory things we were taught and lift our spirits. If we have children or grandchildren, godchildren, nieces, or nephews, these songs are wonderful for us to teach them. Songs of God's love encourage children and stay with us as we grow older.

Prayer: Thank You, Lord, for the gift and blessing of music. I will sing praise to You today. Amen.

Prayers, Thoughts, Gifts of Joy Today:

OCTOBER 9

"So will I sing praise unto thy name forever, that I may daily perform my vows."
-PSALM 61:8

Singing praise to the Lord is good for us, as well as pleasing to Him. In the morning when we rise, if we will make a practice of listening to music that praises God, it will lift our spirit and set a mood of joy and praise for the entire day. Watch—pay special attention to how we begin our day because usually how we start out shines a light on the entire day. Pray before our feet even hit the floor, asking God to bless our day, to help us, to give us wisdom in every task we face, to give us strength to do all we have to do, and pray for others on our prayer list. Then put on praise music and sing praise to Him. Thank Him. Always start the day with a thankful heart.

Prayer: Thank You, Lord, for this new day You have given me. I praise Your name. Make the words of my mouth acceptable to You today. Amen.

Prayers, Thoughts, Gifts of Joy Today:

OCTOBER 10

"The beloved of the Lord shall dwell in safety by him; and the Lord shall cover him all the day long. . . ."

-DEUTERONOMY 33:12

God promises to cover us, to protect us. We shall dwell in safety. This doesn't mean nothing bad will ever happen to us. I believe it is God's promise to us who love Him and have asked Him to be our Lord and Savior that from that moment on, He is with us and protects and shields us. We can feel secure, knowing that no matter what happens around us, we are safe in His hand. He will see us through. We can trust His love and care. David, the one who wrote Psalms, said, "Even though I walk through the valley of the shadow of death, I will fear no evil: for God is with me. . . ." Psalm 23:4. God will go with us through every problem and keep us in His care. If we die, we will go to heaven with Him, so we are okay. Trust.

Prayer: Lord, thank You for giving me security and safety. Thank You for covering me with Your love. Amen.

Prayers, Thoughts, Gifts of Joy Today:

OCTOBER 11

"For our heart shall rejoice in him, because we have trusted in his holy name. Let thy mercy, O Lord, be upon us, according as we hope in thee."

-Psalm 33:21-22

Because of who He is, we can face our life every day because we trust Him. Even when things are not going as we had planned and we feel discouraged, are hurting, sad, and lonely, we can still trust Him. He sees and knows things we don't. He knows what the whole picture is. He may allow us to go through this trial to teach us, to mold us into the person we need to become. We may be going through this because of the consequences of our own or someone else's wrong choices. There are natural consequences to many things in life. When I had to have surgery on my neck for a blockage, I prayed, "Why, Lord?" The answer came to me from God or myself— "Probably because you didn't eat right, exercise, or have a healthy lifestyle." We are quick to blame God, but are we as quick to give Him praise when things go right? When we pray, trust, and put all into His hands, we will be all right.

Prayer: Lord, I rejoice and am glad because of Your salvation and all You have done for me. Thank You. Amen.

Prayers, Thoughts, Gifts of Joy Today:

OCTOBER 12

"And my soul shall be joyful in the Lord: it shall rejoice in his salvation."

-PSALM 35:9

The Bible tells us to rejoice and be joyful over and over again. The Lord evidently likes us to be happy and cheerful. He created us to be happy and joyful. He created us with the ability to laugh and to smile. He gave us the ability to be happy. When we think of the Lord and His salvation, we should rejoice and be glad. We are here to shine this light of happiness and joyfulness on those around us. We are here in this world to be a joyful light.

Prayer: Lord, I rejoice and am glad because of Your salvation and all You have done for me. Thank You. Amen.

Prayers, Thoughts, Gifts of Joy Today:

"Is not the Lord your God with you? . . . now set your heart and your soul to seek the Lord your God."

-1 CHRONICLES 22:18-19

The Lord our God is with us. We should think of Him every morning as we begin our day, throughout our day as we go about living our life, and every night before we go to sleep. Seek His will, ask for His help, and live in His light and direction. In this way, we will be filled with His peace and His joy. When we live believing that God is right there with us through every day, through everything, we can live with a different attitude—one of peace and confidence. God wants us to have His peace and this confidence. He is there with us! God's Word tells us He is with us always.

Prayer: Oh Lord, I thank You for being with me today, for directing my path. I set my heart and my soul to seek Your will for my life today. Amen.

Prayers, Thoughts, Gifts of Joy Today:

OCTOBER 14

"Yet now be strong . . . and be strong, all ye people of the land," saith the Lord, "and work: for I am with you," saith the Lord of hosts.

-HAGGAI 2:4

These words were spoken to people in the Old Testament but can still give us strength today. When we put our trust in the Lord and live according to His will, we can have assurance and be strong. The Bible tells us again and again that He is with us, He gives us strength, He loves us, and cares for us. The above verse also admonishes us to "work." He is with us as we work. Don't just sit and expect Him to do everything for us. He gave us the ability to work, so we are to find our work and do it. Work with our hands or mind, but work. Whatever God has given us the ability to do, do it wholeheartedly.

Prayer: Thank You, Lord, for the ability to work. And let me work for Your honor and glory. Help me to be strong today in all I do. Amen.

Prayers, Thoughts, Gifts of Joy Today:

October 15

"Ah Lord God! Behold, thou hast made the heaven and the earth by thy great power and stretched out arm, and there is nothing too hard for thee."

-JEREMIAH 32:17

God created all the world, all the universe. There is nothing too hard for Him. Nothing! I love these words from the Bible. Why should we, His children, who are loved by Him, ever fear, worry, be anxious, and fret over anything? Grow closer to Him. Study His Word. Pray. Trust. Obey. Live by His teachings. Love. Believe. In this way, our worries and fears will become smaller and will be overcome because we see what He has done and is capable of doing in our lives. When we get our focus off of God, that is when we become weak, fearful, and start doubting Him and ourselves.

Prayer: Lord, it is hard for me to even conceive Your true power and might. My mind cannot fathom the depth and height of Your glory. Help me to trust You and rely on You and not on myself. Help me not to fear. Thank You. Amen.

Prayers, Thoughts, Gifts of Joy Today:

OCTOBER 16

". . . for the Lord seeth not as man seeth; for man looketh on the outside appearance, but the Lord looketh on the heart."

-1 SAMUEL 16:7

Keep our heart with the right spirit and motives. Look to Jesus for our inspiration, to be our guide to live. He knows our heart, our thoughts, our motives and will help us keep our heart right. We should not look at others and see only their outward appearance, but rather, see their inner spirit, their heart. Working on our inner spirit to be closer to God, to make our motives more in keeping with His will, and to do good for Him are good goals for our day. Pray for God's help with all of this daily. Every morning, ask Him to help our hearts be right with Him, and when we pray for this, He will help all of our motives and actions be better. To be a better person inside and to see others for their qualities of heart—rather than just their outside appearance—is what God wants us to do and should be our goal.

Prayer: Lord, help me to keep my heart pure and right in Your sight. When I mess up, open my eyes and heart to see and change my ways. Thank You, Lord. I want to please You. Amen.

Prayers, Thoughts, Gifts of Joy Today:

October 17

"For God so loved the world, that he gave his only begotten Son, that whosoever believeth in him should not perish, but have everlasting life."

-JOHN 3:16

This is a verse many of us memorized as children. It is one of the most power-filled verses in the Bible, showing us the way of salvation—to believe in Jesus Christ. God gave His Son for us as a sacrifice for our sins. Jesus Christ is "the way, the truth, and the light." It is as simple and as difficult as that. "Whosoever believeth in Him should not perish, but have everlasting life." Believe! Often, we think just believing is not enough. We think we have to work or suffer in order to serve God. The Bible tells us "whosoever believes." When we believe, our lives do change. We will want to do good for Him. We will want to be right with God. We will want to serve Him.

Prayer: God, thank You for Jesus, the way to salvation and eternal life. I believe and trust. Thank You for salvation. Amen.

Prayers, Thoughts, Gifts of Joy Today:

OCTOBER 18

"For God sent not his Son into the world to condemn the world; but that the world through him might be saved."

-JOHN 3:17

God loves us and wants to save us. He made the way clear to us. He does not want us to be destroyed or condemned by evil; He wants us to choose light, the right way, and live free. We can only be truly free by God's love. God's love is difficult for us to understand. When we fail Him, we start to feel condemned, but He wants to forgive us and give us His love always. All we have to do is ask for His forgiveness when we fall, and He will forgive us. Jesus Christ's teachings from the Bible talk about love, forgiveness, second chances, hope, joy, peace, strength, and faithfulness. It says God did not send his Son into the world to condemn us, but to save us. What joyful news this is for us!

Prayer: Thank You, God, for Your mercy, Your grace, Your salvation, and love. Amen.

Prayers, Thoughts, Gifts of Joy Today:

OCTOBER 19

"O give thanks unto the Lord, for he is good: for his mercy endureth forever."

-PSALM 107:1

Our Lord is good to us and gives us mercy—not what we deserve. He loves us and cares about us. He created us and knows us. We are His children, and He wants the best for us. We should be so thankful and praise Him for all He has done for us. Become a thankful person. Think on His goodness and mercy to us. Give praise for all things. He is leading us to become the person He always intended us to become. He will help us daily to be that person. Every morning, ask Him to help us to be the person He would have us be, one day at a time.

Prayer: I give my thanks and praise to You, Lord, for ALL You have done, for Your mercy, love, forgiveness, and kindness to me. Help me today to be the person You want me to be. Thank You. Amen.

Prayers, Thoughts, Gifts of Joy Today:

"Truly my soul waiteth upon God: from him cometh my salvation. He only is my rock and my salvation; he is my defense; I shall not be greatly moved."

-PSALM 62:1-2

G od only is my rock and my strong foundation. He is my defense against all forces of harm. I shall not be "greatly" moved. That word greatly made me pause and think. Does this mean I may be shaken up but still stand firm? That is how I took this verse. In life, things come at us, hit us, maybe even knock us down, but because God is our strong foundation—our defender—we will not be greatly moved. We will stand strong again because of God, our salvation, strength, and defense! We will stand strong against the waves that hit us and threaten to knock us off our feet. If we fall down, He will pick us back up and sit us on our solid ground.

Prayer: God, help me to stand strong today. Be my defense, and help me to not be moved. Thank You. Amen.

Prayers, Thoughts, Gifts of Joy Today:

"Blessed be God, even the Father of our Lord Jesus Christ, the Father of mercies, and the God of all comfort. Who comforteth us in all our tribulation, that we may be able to comfort them which are in any trouble, by the comfort wherewith we ourselves are comforted of God."
-2 CORINTHIANS 1:3-4

We will all have problems and troubles at some time in our life. When troubles come, we can pray to God to comfort and help us through. He is faithful to His children and will help us. He may send others to help us through our struggles. We learn and grow through our problems, and one of the things we learn, hopefully, is to reach out to others when you see them going through similar issues. Because we have already been through this, we can help others. God can use us to help each other. This is what He wants us to do—to help others. We are to get outside of ourselves, our own worries and problems, and do for others. Reach out. Pray for them. Do something to help them.

Prayer: Lord, let me see others' pain and comfort them. Let me be willing to help. Thank You. Amen.

Prayers, Thoughts, Gifts of Joy Today:

"Thou art my hiding place and my shield. I hope in thy word."

-PSALM 119:114

God hides us beneath the shelter of His wings, Psalm 17:8 tells us. If you have ever seen a mother hen with her baby chicks, the mother hen does this. The little chicks run to her and get under her wings and are protected, safe, and warm. We can run to God and find safety and refuge from the storms of life. He is our shield and defender. We will find hope in His Word. We can find great strength against troubles by learning to trust Him. Here again is that word "hope" that I love so. With God in our lives, we have great hope. Oh, what peace that should give us. "I hope in Thy word."

Prayer: Thank You, God, for protecting me, for shielding me, for giving me hope. Amen.

Prayers, Thoughts, Gifts of Joy Today:

OCTOBER 23

"Then they cry out unto the Lord in their trouble, and he bringeth them out of their distresses. He maketh the storm a calm, so that the waves thereof are still. Then are they glad because they be quiet; so he bringeth them unto their desired haven."

-PSALM 107:28-30

Keep praying and crying out to the Lord to help in times of trouble. He will hear and quiet the storms of our life. He wants to bring us into calm and safe waters if we will follow and stay close to Him. He will guide us to our desired and safe haven. Trust His unfailing love. He wants to bless us, His children. He wants to bring us out of our distresses. He wants to calm the storms in our life today and make the waves of stress around us be still. He wants us to be glad and peaceful. He wants to bring us to our desired haven.

Prayer: Lord, lead and guide my life. I turn it over to You. I pray and trust in You today. Keep me safe and calm. Keep me calm and at peace, even when I am in the midst of a storm in my life. Thank You. Amen.

Prayers, Thoughts, Gifts of Joy Today:

OCTOBER 24

**"Be not afraid nor dismayed . . . for the battle is
not yours, but God's."**

-2 CHRONICLES 20:15

Don't worry or be afraid; God is in control. No matter
how bad it seems to us today, the battle is His. We can
look at the world around us, with all its problems, and lose
heart or become discouraged and afraid. Or we can look to
God instead of the world, instead of our problems, instead of
people who may fail us. He is greater and bigger than these.
"The battle is not yours, but God's." Remember this. He is
more than able. Pray and stay in a right place with Him. Ask
Him to fight the battle for us.

Prayer: Lord, I know You are in control, not me. Help me
to remain strong in this battle. Keep me safe in Your arms.
Fight for me. Thank You. Amen.

Prayers, Thoughts, Gifts of Joy Today:

OCTOBER 25

"I wait for the Lord, my soul doth wait, and in his word do I hope."

-PSALM 130:5

What does it mean to wait on the Lord? To me, it means praying about everything and seeking His wisdom and guidance. It means not going rashly ahead, quickly making decisions without thought of what He would want us to do, only thinking of what we want. James 1:5 says, "If any of you lack wisdom, let him ask of God . . . and it shall be given." Waiting is not something we like to do, is it? No. Most of us are not good at being patient. God tells us in His Word to wait and to hope. Trust Him today. Wait and hope!

Prayer: Lord, I do hope and trust in You. Give me the wisdom to know when to be still and wait and when to act and go forward. Thank You for always being there when I call out. Amen.

Prayers, Thoughts, Gifts of Joy Today:

OCTOBER 26

"Thou shalt weep no more: he will be very gracious unto thee at the voice of thy cry; when he shall hear it, he will answer thee."

-ISAIAH **30:19**

The Lord hears our cries, knows our hearts, our cares, our brokenheartedness and cares when we cry out to Him for help. He will be there for us in our times of distress and hurt. He will answer our prayers. His answer may not always be the answer we want—and He may not answer us as quickly as we would wish—but we need to trust that He knows what is best for us. The best for us may hurt at this time. He sees and knows things we do not. This earthly life is not the end. He sees eternity, which is much bigger. Let us try to look with new eyes at our problems, the things that are bothering us right now. When we look at these from God's point of view, they may dim or grow smaller.

Prayer: O Lord, thank You for hearing me when I cry to you and for caring for me. Let me trust You more and let go of my own issues. I put my life in Your hands. You know what is best for me. Help me accept this. Amen.

Prayers, Thoughts, Gifts of Joy Today:

OCTOBER 27

"I have set the Lord always before me; because he is at my right hand, I shall not be moved."
-PSALM 16:8

When we think about God, pray, and read His Word, He is there right beside us and will keep us stable and strong in our walk with Him. We will not be easily swayed by the winds of doubt, fear, or mistrust because we have read and meditated on His promises to us. He is our hope and our stay. Circumstances will not move our firm foundation, which is Jesus Christ. When we set the Lord always before us, we put Him first and trust His will for our lives. We will be less likely to make decisions that are based only on our own wants when we do this. By putting God before us, we are saying we want to live the way He would have us live.

Prayer: Be at my right hand today, Lord. Keep me in Your care. Keep me strong. You are my hope and my stay. Lead me to live the way You would have me live. Thank You. Amen.

Prayers, Thoughts, Gifts of Joy Today:

OCTOBER 28

"Say to them that are of a fearful heart, be strong, fear not."

-Isaiah 35:4

Be strong and do not be afraid! This is difficult sometimes, isn't it? There are times when we feel strong and fearless, but much of the time, we are weak and fearful, full of doubts and worries. Doubts in ourselves and in those around us overwhelm us. For me, the only way to face life strong and fearless is through the power of prayer and reading God's Word. We can trust Him to help us daily through this thing called life. Memorize scriptures of courage, such as, "I can do all things through Christ who strengthens me," Phil. 4:13 and, "In all things, we are more than conquerors through Him that loves us." When we start feeling inadequate, repeat these verses and others like them over and over. This will help to give us power.

Prayer: Lord, help me to stay strong and fearless right now. Thank You. Amen.

Prayers, Thoughts, Gifts of Joy Today:

OCTOBER 29

**"If ye have faith as a grain of mustard seed . . .
nothing shall be impossible unto you."**
-MATTHEW 17:20

Faith—complete trust, confidence, and belief in God. Even a tiny, true faith can accomplish unbelievable things. Trust, have faith, believe, and pray. The Bible says, "Nothing shall be impossible for you." Of course, we don't need to take this verse out of context. Nothing goes against God's principles and His teachings. This verse doesn't mean we can pray for anything and just get it. When we have true faith, we will be praying for God's will, not for things contrary to His will. If it is in His will, it will be possible for us.

Prayer: Thank You for Your encouraging Word. Thank You for the power You give me through prayer. Give me wisdom when I pray, and I ask that You keep me in Your will for my life. Amen.

Prayers, Thoughts, Gifts of Joy Today:

OCTOBER 30

"For the Lord God is a sun and shield: the Lord will give grace and glory: no good thing will he withhold from them that walk uprightly."

-PSALM 84:11

The Lord our God is like the sun. He shines His light so we can see. He is a shield who defends us. He loves us and shows grace: His unearned favor. He gives us glory, which is high renown and honor. He withholds nothing of worth from us, but wishes to give us all good things. The Bible teaches us these truths. We are blessed by Him daily. Even when we are going through struggles, heartaches, and problems, He is there right beside us. We have to keep on trusting and keep on believing. Hold on to His strong hand.

Prayer: Thank You, God, for all Your many blessings in my life. I am so grateful. I know You will withhold nothing good from me. Thank You. Amen.

Prayers, Thoughts, Gifts of Joy Today:

"And be renewed in the spirit of your mind."
-EPHESIANS 4:23

What we think about and dwell on, we will become. Be renewed in mind and spirit today, right now, by reading God's Word, praying, and thinking on Him. We can renew our spirit with God's help. Become enthusiastic and optimistic because we know the final victory belongs to the Lord! Do not allow worry, frustration, and sadness to weigh us down and become a way of daily life for us. Instead, be renewed daily by God's Spirit. Ask and we will receive.

Prayer: Lord, remove this worry, these problems, this feeling of nervousness and doubt from me right now. Fill me up with Your Spirit of love, joy, and hope. Thank You. Amen.

Prayers, Thoughts, Gifts of Joy Today:

November 1

"And his disciples came to him, and awoke him, saying, Lord, save us: we perish. And he saith unto them, why are ye fearful, O ye of little faith? Then he arose, and rebuked the winds and the sea: and there was a great calm."

-Matthew 8:25-26

Sometimes we feel that the storms of our life are going to kill us, don't we? The waves hit us, knock us down, and threaten to pull us under, but our Lord is there for us. All we have to do is call out to Him to calm these storms. He can calm even the greatest, strongest storm. Have faith and believe. Rely upon Him to calm these storms this very moment. Lean on Jesus in trust and hope. He will give us a great calm. He wants us to learn to depend on Him through our struggles. Letting go of our sense of control can be hard for us. We want to "fix" things for ourselves and others, but sometimes we just can't. By letting go of the problem and giving it to God, He can bring us a great calm within our very being.

Prayer: Oh Lord, calm this storm in my life right now. Quiet me. Bring me peace. Quiet. Calm. Rest. Trust. Thank You, Jesus. Amen.

Prayers, Thoughts, Gifts of Joy Today:

NOVEMBER 2

"Be not afraid, only believe."

-MARK 5:36

God doesn't want us to be afraid. Over and over, throughout the Bible, there are verses that say "fear not," "don't be anxious," and "don't be afraid." Believe that God is able and will take care of us. Trust Him. Read His Word more often; this very act will give us strength and encouragement. His promises to us are uplifting and life enhancing. With Him by our side, we can face today and tomorrow without fear. "Be not afraid, only believe." It is our nature to be afraid when we don't understand exactly what is happening to us or why. When we trust God, we have to believe that He is in control, and whatever is happening will come out okay because He is there for us.

Prayer: Thank You, Lord, for Your care and love. I believe and trust You to help me through this day and my tomorrows as well. I can do ALL things. I can get through this because You are my strength!!! Amen.

Prayers, Thoughts, Gifts of Joy Today:

NOVEMBER 3

"Draw near to God, and he will draw near to you."

-JAMES **4:8**

Spending time with Jesus will bring us nearer to Him. As we pray and read His Word, memorize verses to strengthen us, and study His Word, all these things will draw us closer. He will be near to us when we seek to know and do His will for our lives. God wants to live daily with us, blessing us, keeping us in His care. I read a saying, "If you don't feel close to God, guess who moved?" It is not God who moves away from us but we who pull away from Him. Move back closer, nearer! Just as in life, when we spend time with someone, we become closer to them, and they become more dear and precious to us. It is so with our God. If we love Him, we will want to spend time with Him.

Prayer: Lord, keep me near Your heart. There is peace and safety there, love and care. Thank You. Amen.

Prayers, Thoughts, Gifts of Joy Today:

NOVEMBER 4

". . . attend to my words; incline thine ear unto my sayings. Let them not depart from thine eyes; keep them in the midst of thine heart."
-PROVERBS 4:21-22

Pay attention to God's Word. It will strengthen us, guide us, and help us to make it through this life. He wants us to be fulfilled and have purpose. Only through Him can we be truly fulfilled, content, and happy. He created each of us for a life purpose. To find fulfillment, we must pay attention to His Words, and keep His teachings and precepts in our heart. Every morning, we should pray and ask God to show us what He would have us do this day. When we pray this prayer, we will become more aware of our words and our deeds. We will pay closer attention to our actions that speak so much louder than what we say. How we treat those around us in this life says much about our hearts. Watch our attitudes and actions closely. With God's help, we will become a better person and shine for Him.

Prayer: Lord, let me keep Your Word ever in my heart so that I might live every day fulfilling the purposes You have for me. Keep my heart, my words, and my actions pure. Thank You. Amen.

Prayers, Thoughts, Gifts of Joy Today:

"I am come a light into the world, that whosoever believeth in me should not abide in darkness."

-John 12:46

Live in the light of Jesus Christ. He came to bring light into the world. He opens our eyes and our hearts to the light. Pray and ask Him to shine His light on us and through us today. We are here in this world to reflect His glory and light all around us. We do this by being loving, kind, giving, sharing, speaking kind words, and doing good to others as we go along daily. May we shine His light through our life today! May others see us and think well of Jesus Christ. We never want to bring shame or dishonor to His name.

Prayer: Lord, let me shine brightly for You today. May all I do, think, or say reflect Your love. Thank You. Amen.

Prayers, Thoughts, Gifts of Joy Today:

NOVEMBER 6

"But whoso hearkeneth unto me shall dwell safely, and shall be quiet from fear of evil."
-PROVERBS 1:33

Listen to and learn from God's Word. When we live our lives according to His teachings, we can feel more secure and have peace. Trusting in God to take care of us and to keep us from evil is a peaceful way in which to live. This doesn't mean nothing bad will ever happen to us, but we will dwell in God's care, and He will care for us no matter what is going on around us. He will hold our hand and give us quiet from the fear of evil. This is so important in today's world. We listen to the news or read about things that are happening in the world, and we can become fearful of the evil going on around us. God gives us assurance that we can dwell in safety when we listen to Him and live according to His teachings. We don't have to fear evil, for He is with us.

Prayer: Lord, when I am afraid, give me quiet and safety; let me know You are with me. Thank You. Amen.

Prayers, Thoughts, Gifts of Joy Today:

NOVEMBER 7

"Thy word have I hid in my heart, that I might not sin against thee."

-PSALM 119:11

We should memorize precious scriptures so that in times of distress or joy, we can recall them and quote them aloud to ourselves so they will uplift and encourage us. Scriptures can give great comfort to our lives. Read them, study them, and hide them in our hearts by memorizing. This will do us a great service throughout our life. If we have children, grandchildren, nieces, or nephews, we should read scriptures to them when they are young and teach them to learn scriptures. This will bless us and them throughout life. The Word of God is a must for us to read and learn. His Word, hidden in our hearts, will help us to do the right thing.

Prayer: Thank You, God, for Your wonderful Words. Help me to hide more of them in my heart. Help me to think on the scriptures and recall them in times of stress as well as times of joy. Amen.

Prayers, Thoughts, Gifts of Joy Today:

November 8

**"He layeth up sound wisdom for the righteous:
he is a buckler to them that walk uprightly."**
-Proverbs 2:7

The definition of buckler is a shield, so this helps us understand this verse a bit better. God is a shield, a defender of those who try to walk and live right. He also will give us wisdom as we try to live uprightly. He alone causes us to be strong and stand firm against wrong. Trust Him to help us today to have wisdom and strength. We do not need to be fearful. God is with us. He is our shield. He is our defender. He is our daily help as we walk through this life. He will give us sound wisdom when we ask Him.

Prayer: God, I pray for Your sound wisdom and Your shield of protection in my life today. As I go about my way, be with me. Thank You. Amen.

Prayers, Thoughts, Gifts of Joy Today:

NOVEMBER 9

> "Grace be unto you, and peace, from God our Father, and from the Lord Jesus Christ. I thank my God upon every remembrance of you, always in every prayer of mine for you all making request with joy."
>
> -PHILIPPIANS 1:2-4

The above verses are a wonderful prayer or greeting to someone. I often use this verse in a note or card to someone. It is a blessing from the Word of God. We ask God to give them grace (the free and unmerited favor of God). We ask Him to give them peace. We thank God for them in our lives. We make our request for them with joy in our hearts because God is listening to us. It is a wonderful thing to write notes of encouragement or verses like this to people who mean something to our lives. It is good for us to let others know how important they are to us and to appreciate them. Today, think of someone who has been special to your life and write them a note of blessing and thanks.

Prayer: Lord, thank You for those who bless my life. I lift them up to You today, and ask in joy that You bless them. Thank You. Amen.

Prayers, Thoughts, Gifts of Joy Today:

NOVEMBER 10

"Let all those that put their trust in thee rejoice: let them ever shout for joy because thou defendest them: let them also that love thy name be joyful in thee."

-PSALM 5:11

Rejoice and be filled with joy because we trust and love the Lord. He defends us. He loves and cares for us. Today we can stand firm because of whose we are. He is our Savior, our Lord. He gives us joy and rejoicing! Hallelujah! We should be thankful and praise His name because of all He has done for us.

Express gratitude and thankfulness daily. When we live in a state of gratefulness, we are more joyful. Let's go about our day today thinking of all that God has done for us and being thankful for what He is doing now—right now!

Prayer: Lord, I trust in You. I love Your name. Let me rejoice and be joyful today. Thank You for the joy You give. Amen.

Prayers, Thoughts, Gifts of Joy Today:

"For thou, Lord, wilt bless the righteous; with
favor wilt thou compass him as with a shield."
-PSALM 5:12

The Lord is our blessing and our shield. He blesses us with all manner of good things every day. Even when we are dealing with problems and heartaches, He is with us, shielding us from the worst and helping us to stand strong. We can be strong because God is by our side, helping us daily. When we feel defeated and low, pray to God for strength and His blessings. We will receive. We can take our burdens to Him and leave them at His feet.

"Doing the best we can, we live with joy and
freedom."
-NORMAN VINCENT PEALE

Prayer: Oh Lord, thank You for your blessings, Your favor, Your shield around me today. I praise Your name. I will fear no evil for You are with me. Help me to bring my burdens to You and leave them in Your capable hands. You are able to handle this! Thank You. Amen.

Prayers, Thoughts, Gifts of Joy Today:

NOVEMBER 12

"My help cometh from the Lord, which made heaven and earth. He will not suffer thy foot to be moved: he that keepeth thee will not slumber."

-PSALM 121:2-3

"Go to sleep in peace. God is awake."

-VICTOR HUGO

We can sleep in peace because we know God is in control. He is our help in times of trouble and distress. He is bigger than our fears and worries. We can trust Him to handle "this." Pray. Breathe. Relax. Put everything into His capable hands. Give it all to God who loves and cares about us.

Prayer: Oh Lord, I trust in You. I believe in You. I know You can handle these problems and my entire life. Help me, I pray, to have peace and trust You even more. Thank You. Amen.

Prayers, Thoughts, Gifts of Joy Today:

November 13

"I love them that love me; and those that seek me early shall find me."

-Proverbs 8:17

The above verse is speaking of wisdom and understanding. We should pray for and seek wisdom. One of our prayers every morning should be for the Lord to give us wisdom for the day before us. Sometimes our own self gets in the way, and ill-advised thinking or words come from our mouth that are not very wise. But when we begin our day by asking God to guard our heart, mind, and mouth—and grant us understanding and wisdom—we will discover that life goes much smoother.

Prayer: God, grant me understanding and wisdom today. "May the words of my mouth and the meditation of my heart be acceptable in Your sight." Thank You. Amen.

Prayers, Thoughts, Gifts of Joy Today:

"When I consider thy heavens, the work of thy fingers, the moon and the stars, which thou hast ordained; what is man, that thou are mindful of him? . . . O Lord, our Lord, how excellent is thy name in all the earth!"

-PSALM 8:3-4 & 9

Go outside this week at night and look up at the moon and the stars. Stand in awe and wonder at all the Lord God made. Think about mankind and how very small we are in comparison, yet God created all the world and gave it to us. That a God this powerful and majestic would love us and think of us is beyond our comprehension. His name is excellent, and we should praise and thank Him. Celebrate this. Be filled with Thanksgiving!!!

"Create celebrations in each day. Live well."

-ALEXANDRA STODDARD

Prayer: Thank You, Lord, for giving me life, for giving me the moon, stars, and the heavens above to see and enjoy. You are excellent. You are powerful. You are my God, and I thank You and praise You. Amen.

Prayers, Thoughts, Gifts of Joy Today:

NOVEMBER 15

> **"As ye have therefore received Christ Jesus the Lord, so walk ye in him. Rooted and built up in him, and established in the faith, as ye have been taught, abounding therein with thanksgiving."**
> **-COLOSSIANS 2:6-7**

B e built up, walk with Christ in His way, and be established (set, fixed, recognized) in the faith. Always be thankful, recognizing all He has done for us. To abound in thankfulness means we should always be aware of God's grace and mercy to us and thank Him daily.

I love the season of Thanksgiving. The smells, the tastes, the fellowship, the joy this season brings excite me. Make a new tradition of celebrating and being thankful each day of the Thanksgiving season by writing down things for which we are thankful and will celebrate. Celebrate every day by lighting a candle and saying a prayer of thankfulness for this gift, this blessing in our lives.

Prayer: Lord, thank You for Your mercy, grace, love, and salvation. I am blessed by You. Thank You today for ———————————————————. Amen.

Prayers, Thoughts, Gifts of Joy Today:

NOVEMBER 16

"Ask, and it shall be given you; seek, and ye shall find; knock, and it shall be opened unto you."
-MATTHEW 7:7

We are to pray and ask our Heavenly Father for whatever it is we want. This verse isn't a blanket "ask for it and get it" answer. We often take a verse out of all the others and stand on that one verse. Have we read all the verses in the Bible and learned God's principles and teachings? When we do this, then we will pray specifically for what we want, but we will add "if this is Your will for me right now, Lord." Sometimes what we think we want would not be the best for us at this time in our life. If it is in God's will, then yes, we want it for our lives because we believe His will is the best for us always. When we pray, we should ask for God's will. If we pray with His principles and teachings from the Bible in our mind, we can pray as He would want us to pray and be more clear in our wants.

Prayer: Lord, give me the wisdom to pray in Your will, to want the things You would have for me, the best things for me. Thank You for all You have given me already. Let me live today in thankfulness. Thank You. Amen.

Prayers, Thoughts, Gifts of Joy Today:

November 17

"Love your enemies, bless them that curse you, do good to them that hate you, and pray for them which despitefully use you, and persecute you."

-Matthew 5:44

O h, this verse is a difficult one—but one we need to read often and take to heart. In life, there will be those people who mistreat us and we feel do us wrong. It is hard, but God tells us to pray for them, to care about them, and to ask His blessings on them. I am not saying this is easy, but it is the best for us. When we harbor hatred and do not forgive, it hurts our own health. We must try to let it all go, pray for those who treat us badly, and leave them up to God. Ask God to bless them in our prayers and then move on. I have to work on this one myself, but I know it is the right thing to do.

Prayer: Lord, when others hurt me or my loved ones, help me to let this go and not dwell on it. Give me instead Your Spirit of love and kindness. Help me to shine Your light and do the right thing. Thank You for helping me with this. Amen.

Prayers, Thoughts, Gifts of Joy Today:

NOVEMBER 18

". . . He inclined unto me, and heard my cry. He brought me up also out of a horrible pit, out of the miry clay, and set my feet upon a rock and established my goings. And he hath put a new song in my mouth, even praise unto our God."
-PSALM 40:1-3

Pray. Ask God for help. He will hear a sincere prayer. He can take something horrible and make it good for us. He can lift us out of all the "stuff," set our feet on firm ground, and establish our life. He will put a new song in our heart, and we will praise Him again. When we go through a terrible ordeal, a bad time in our life, a tragedy, we can call out to God and He will hear our cry. He will bring us out of this time in our life if we allow Him to do so. There have been times in my life when I thought nothing good would ever come to me again. With God, good did come again. Oh, that doesn't mean I didn't go through the bad, but God brought me through to the other side, held me through this, and set my feet upon solid ground again. Praise Him for His help in our lives and lean on Him always.

Prayer: Lord, help me in dealing with _____. Raise me up. Place my feet on solid ground. Give me a new song in my heart and mouth today. I will give You all the glory and praise for what You are doing and what You have done. Thank You. Amen.

Prayers, Thoughts, Gifts of Joy Today:

". . . if any man minister; let him do it as of the ability which God giveth: that God in all things may be glorified through Jesus Christ, to whom be praise and dominion forever and ever. Amen."
-1 PETER 4:11

When we attend to the needs of someone or do something to help another, we are ministering to them. We should do this to bring glory and honor to God, not to ourselves. God gives each of us an ability, a talent, to be used for His glory. Give Him the praise and honor. We may not think we have a "talent," but the Bible teaches us that God gives to each a talent to be used for Him. We may have the voice of encouragement, we may play an instrument, be able to sing, be able to speak well, write, create, paint, garden, cook, clean, have a brain for math or science, be a good listener, be a professional who has a talent for making money, be full of charity for others, or give our time and efforts to help others. Let Him use us today. Let us give Him our time and talents, whatever those talents are.

"Be the reason someone smiles today."
-ANONYMOUS

Prayer: Lord, thank You for my abilities. Let me use my gifts, my talents to honor and glorify You. To You be all the praise, glory, and honor. Amen.

Prayers, Thoughts, Gifts of Joy Today:

"O give thanks unto the Lord; for he is good: because his mercy endureth forever."
-PSALM 118:1

Give thanks, honor, and glory to God for His goodness, love, and mercy to us. In this special season of Thanksgiving, we usually pay attention to all of our blessings. Hopefully, we will teach our children or loved ones to be more thankful—even after the season—if we have the opportunity. At every meal, we usually bow our heads and thank God for our food and blessings. This is good. We also should bow our heads and pray throughout the day and night whenever we think on God's goodness to us. Let us not become complacent and forget to be thankful for our many blessings. I try to write down blessings throughout my day so as to notice and bring my attention to them more fully. When we get into the habit of noticing blessings, we will see so many and they will become abundantly clear to us. We should also seek to be a blessing ourselves to others throughout our day. Try to bless someone today as we go about our daily activities.

Prayer: O Lord, my heart is full of thankfulness this morning to You for all my many blessings. I thank You for Your mercy and love to me. I am grateful. Let me share my blessings with those with whom I come in contact today, and let me bless them. Thank You. Amen.

Prayers, Thoughts, Gifts of Joy Today:

November 21

"The Lord is nigh unto all them that call upon him, to all that call upon him in truth."

-Psalm 145:18

The Lord is close at hand to all of us who call out to Him. He knows our hearts and when we are sincere. It is a wonderful blessing to have a Heavenly Father who hears us when we pray sincerely to Him. He is there when we reach out for His help, His forgiveness, His love, and His ever-present being. Oh how thankful always we should be to Him. It is an amazing thing to realize the God who created us is near to us when we call on Him. He created prayer so that we have direct access to Him, day or night. All we have to do is say "Oh God," and He is there for us.

Prayer: Thank You, Heavenly Father, that You are near me and hear my sincere prayers. You, Almighty God, are close to me. That amazes me. I humbly come to You, thanking You for all You have done. Amen.

Prayers, Thoughts, Gifts of Joy Today:

"O satisfy us early with thy mercy; that we may rejoice and be glad all our days."

-PSALM 90:14

We ask God to be merciful, to have compassion and forgive us when we do not even deserve it. When we receive mercy, we can rejoice and live happily because of God's goodness toward us. We should be thankful and glad due to God's mercy and favor. Rejoice, be glad, be thankful. Love God and be blessed. He wants us to be glad all our days. This is encouraging to me. Some people think of God as judgmental and condemning, but if we will read the Bible—all of it—we will see a God of mercy, love, forgiveness, and compassion who wants to give us joy and gladness all of our days. He wants only the best for us and delights in giving us His blessings.

Prayer: Thank You, God, for Your mercy, Your love, and Your blessings to me this day. I will rejoice and be glad because of what You have done. Thank You. Amen.

Prayers, Thoughts, Gifts of Joy Today:

November 23

"And offer a sacrifice of thanksgiving. . . ."

-Amos 4:5

Sacrifice may mean a surrendering of thanksgiving. When we offer our thanksgiving to the Lord, we humbly come before Him, thanking Him sincerely for all He has done, realizing that without Him, we would be nothing, we would have nothing. We surrender our praise and thanks to Him. In this season of Thanksgiving, let us consider our thanks, our true heart in this matter. Do we sacrifice (surrender) our thanks to God? Are we thankful to Him as much as we should be? Pray, bow before Him, praise, honor, and thank Him today. Come before Him humbly and with a thankful heart.

Prayer: Oh God, my God, without You, I am nothing. I have nothing except from You. Thank You for my life, my days upon this earth, and Your love and care for me. Thank You is not enough, but it is my sacrifice of praise and thankfulness to You today. Amen.

Prayers, Thoughts, Gifts of Joy Today:

NOVEMBER 24

"That I may publish with the voice of thanks-giving and tell of all thy wondrous works."
-PSALM 26:7

B e thankful and tell others what God has done for us. Be bold to praise Him. Let our voice speak out in true thanks-giving for all He has done for us through this past year and for what He will do through the year ahead. Without Him, our lives would be a mess. Praise, be grateful, and be thankful today and always! We should live in a state of thanksgiving, and in this special Thanksgiving season, this gift of thanksgiving should be ever on our lips to give to the Lord. By showing our thankfulness, we can teach our children, our grandchildren, and those around us to show their thankfulness, too.

Prayer: Oh Lord, I am so very thankful and filled with praise today for all of Your blessings, mercy, and love to me. Bless my family today and in the coming year. Let us all bless You with our lives. We cannot live without Your blessing on us. Thank You. Amen.

Prayers, Thoughts, Gifts of Joy Today:

NOVEMBER 25

"How excellent is thy loving kindness, O God! Therefore, the children of men put their trust under the shadow of thy wings."

-PSALM 36:7

The Lord our God loves us and protects us. We can find shelter from the evils of life. We are safe because of God's loving kindness to us. Run to Him today, asking for His help. We should put our faith and trust in Him. We can feel secure because He is there for us every minute of every day. Read His Word and pray. These two things will make us stronger, whatever we may face. Trust and have faith even when darkness surrounds us.

"Faith is the bird that feels the light and sings while the dawn is still dark."

-RADINDRANATH TEGORE

Prayer: Thank You for Your loving kindness and Your shelter for me. I run to You and am safe and secure from the storms of life. Because of You, I can feel secure, even while enduring the darkness. Thank You. Amen.

Prayers, Thoughts, Gifts of Joy Today:

"Which of you by taking thought can add one cubit unto his stature? . . . Therefore, take no thought, saying, What shall we eat? Or, What shall we drink? Or, wherewithal shall we be clothed? . . . for your Heavenly Father knoweth that ye have need of all these things. But seek ye first the kingdom of God, and his righteousness; and all these things shall be added unto you. Take therefore no thought for the morrow. . . ."

-MATTHEW 6:27-31, 34

Don't worry about things. God is in control—not us. Think about God and His will for us, pray and ask for His help. Then rest in His Word that He will take care of us. I do not think these verses mean not to work, not to make intelligent plans for our future. To me, it says don't worry, don't stress over things beyond our control. Rest in the Lord. He knows what we need. Often, we miss much good and joy in our lives because we are worrying needlessly about tomorrow, what might or might not happen. Worrying never helps anyone or anything.

Prayer: Lord, thank You for theses verses. Help me to rest in You, to trust in You, and not to worry, but do the best I can, with Your help, and leave the rest up to You. Thank You. Amen.

Prayers, Thoughts, Gifts of Joy Today:

NOVEMBER 27

> ". . . in everything by prayer and supplication with thanksgiving let your request be made known unto God."
>
> -PHILIPPIANS 4:6

The first part of this verse says, "Be careful for nothing. . . ." Another translation says, "Be anxious about nothing. . . ." So don't worry about anything, but pray and ask God about whatever is going on. Always have thanks and gratefulness when we pray. The Bible teaches throughout for us to be thankful, grateful, appreciative, and thoughtful as we come to our God with prayers and supplications (asking and begging for). The Bible teaches us that He loves us and wants to give us good things. We pray to thank Him, to ask for His help in our lives, and for His blessings. He hears us when we pray.

Prayer: Thank You, God, for hearing my prayers. Give me wisdom to know better how to pray. Amen.

Prayers, Thoughts, Gifts of Joy Today:

"Beloved, let us love one another: for love is of God; and every one that loveth is born of God, and knoweth God. He that loveth not knoweth not God; for God is love. In this was manifested the love of God toward us, because that God sent his only begotten Son into the world, that we might live through him."

-1 JOHN 4:7-9

What we do speaks much louder than what we say. How we treat others speaks volumes about our hearts. Watch our hearts and motives closely. When we are not in a loving spirit, we are out of sorts with God because God is love and love is of God. God wants us to love others and live with love through His strength. Sometimes people are unlovable, but we should strive to love them in His power, not our own. We may disagree with someone, not accept their behavior and their choices, but we are still to love them. This is difficult at times. God will help us if we ask for His help in this. This does not mean we have to roll over and be passive about everything we hold dear: our faith, our beliefs, or our values. It does mean we will behave in a loving, kind way with a spirit of grace and gentleness that God gives, even when we are disagreeing.

Prayer: Lord, help me to love others through Your power, even those I don't always like. Thank You for loving me and being kind to me even when I didn't deserve Your love. Amen.

Prayers, Thoughts, Gifts of Joy Today:

NOVEMBER 29

"Help us, O God of our salvation, for the glory of thy name: and deliver us, and purge away our sins, for thy name's sake."

-PSALM 79:9

Let us live right and do good works so that the name of God might be lifted up and glorified. He is our help, our salvation, and any good we might accomplish is due to Him. Give Him all the glory and honor. We are His creation, His workmanship. Pray that He will use us to glorify Himself more. Lift up the name of Jesus Christ today. In all we do and say, think about how our words and actions reflect on God. Before we open our mouths to speak, think. My daddy put a sign up at his workshop that said "Think!" He was doing this for us kids to remind us to think before we did anything stupid.

Prayer: Lord, help me to live today in such a way that I will bring glory and honor to Your name. Let me not fail You or bring any shame upon You. Let me think before I do anything "stupid." Thank You. Amen.

Prayers, Thoughts, Gifts of Joy Today:

NOVEMBER 30

**"And the Lord, he it is that doth go before thee;
he will be with thee, he will not fail thee, neither
forsake thee: fear not, neither be dismayed."**

H e goes with us. He is with us. He will not fail us. He will
not forsake us. He knows who we are, and He knows
what we need. We should never be afraid because we have a
God who gives us these promises. We should not be discouraged, down, or depressed when we think on these promises.
This is a great verse to commit to memory and recall in times
when we need reminding: "Fear not—neither be dismayed."
Why? Because God, the all-powerful One, is with us! He goes
ahead of us and stays with us.

Prayer: Thank You, Lord, for these precious promises
from Your Word. I will not be afraid or discouraged today
because You go before me and are with me. When I look
at circumstances, I sometimes become afraid or discouraged. But when I look to You, I no longer fear. Thank You.
Amen.

Prayers, Thoughts, Gifts of Joy Today:

DECEMBER 1

"And she shall bring forth a son, and thou shalt call his name Jesus: for he shall save his people from their sins."

-MATTHEW 1:21

"He shall save his people from their sins." We can breathe a sigh of relief, even during this busy season when, and if, we will focus on Jesus. Christmas is the most glorious time of the year to me. I love the whole season, so full of joy and love. It can also be a sad time for many, so we should be even more loving and thoughtful of others. Bless God and bless others as we go about our day today. Notice our face; put on a smile of joy. Notice our words that they are kind, loving, and good. Notice how we react and treat others who come into our paths today. Treat them with love and compassion. They may be having a bad day, but our reaction or treatment of them can change their entire day. Our sins are forgiven by Jesus Christ. We should be happy today.

Prayer: Thank You, God, for saving my soul. Thank You for Jesus and this Christmas season of celebration and joy. Let me bless You and others today. Merry Christmas!!! Amen.

Prayers, Thoughts, Gifts of Joy Today:

DECEMBER 2

**". . . and they shall call his name Emmanuel,
which being interpreted is, God with us."**
-MATTHEW 1:23

How wonderful and marvelous to think about God coming in the form of man to be with us, to understand us, to go through all the human things we do. He is with us. God is with us! He knows us, understands us, and loves us. During this busy season of celebration, let us remember every day why we are joyous and celebrating. "Jesus is the reason for the season." Let us celebrate and be joyous. With God with us, we can do this!

Prayer: That you came to be with us, God, amazes me. I cannot even imagine or comprehend how or why You did this, but I am thankful. Let me remember every day the real reason for Christmas-the true Christmas; let me hold it in my heart. Thank You. Amen.

Prayers, Thoughts, Gifts of Joy Today:

DECEMBER 3

"When they saw the star, they rejoiced with exceeding great joy."

-MATTHEW 2:10

When the wise men saw the star that led them to Jesus, they rejoiced with exceeding great joy, and likewise, we should rejoice. Jesus gives us our joy. He is the reason for the season of celebration. Oh come and let us worship Him today and all during this season of celebration of His birth. To live each day with exceeding great joy is a fabulous way to live and celebrate Him. God wants us to have joy in our hearts and our lives. He created joy. He gives it to us.

We should never be sad and discouraged for any length of time because He came to give us exceeding great joy! We may have a hard time during the holidays because someone we loved is no longer with us, or something has changed in our lives that makes celebration and joy hard. Life gets difficult sometimes. God is still with us. He hasn't left us, no matter what. Ask Him for His joy in our hearts today.

Prayer: God, give me Your exceeding great joy in my heart today. Let my heart overflow with Your love, peace, and great joy. Thank You. Amen.

Prayers, Thoughts, Gifts of Joy Today:

DECEMBER 4

"For unto us a child is born, unto us a son is given: and the government shall be upon his shoulder: and his name shall be called Wonderful, Counsellor, The Mighty God, The Everlasting Father, The Prince of Peace."

-ISAIAH 9:6

W onderful, Counsellor, The Mighty God, The Everlasting Father, and The Prince of Peace. What glorious names for our Savior, Jesus Christ! He is the reason we celebrate Christmas. Celebrate His love, His peace, His joy—all He has done and all He keeps doing in our lives. Play some joyful, worshipful Christmas music and sing along today. This will bless us when we do. It is good to sing along and praise Jesus at this special time of year, and who doesn't love Christmas carols? Have joy in our world today!!! Make joy all around. Think about joy, what we love about this season, and then do it. Do we love Christmas music, the decorations, the food, the smell of cedar or pine, friends or family getting together for a meal? Find ways in which to celebrate and bring joy into our lives and the lives of others and then share that joy with all those around.

Prayer: Lord, I worship and praise Your glorious name today. Thank You for all You are: Wonderful, Counsellor, The Mighty God, The Everlasting Father, The Prince of Peace. Marvelous is Your Holy name! Amen and Amen.

Prayers, Thoughts, Gifts of Joy Today:

DECEMBER 5

"God also hath highly exalted him, and given him a name which is above every name: that at the name of Jesus every knee should bow, of things in heaven and things in earth, and things under the earth; and that every tongue should confess that Jesus Christ is Lord, to the glory of God the Father."

-PHILIPPIANS 2:9-11

Jesus is the name above all other names. We should take His name seriously and respect it always. One day, we will stand before Him, fall to our knees, and bow before Him in awe and worship. On that day, we will give Him praise. We should give Him our praise now, this day, as well. We should never take His name lightly and never curse using the precious name of Jesus. We should revere the name of Jesus and hold it in the highest esteem and honor. It is a precious name—a name above all other names. It is the most important name we will ever know.

Prayer: Praise and glory, honor, worship, love, and respect I give You, Jesus, my Lord and my God. Thank You is not enough, but always I give You my thanks. Amen.

Prayers, Thoughts, Gifts of Joy Today:

DECEMBER 6

"And Mary said, my soul doth magnify the Lord, and my spirit hath rejoiced in God my Savior."
-LUKE 1:46-47

We, as Mary, should lift up and magnify the Lord Jesus Christ. He should be magnified and we ourselves should become less. It is our human nature to think of ourselves, and we can become easily distracted—especially during the Christmas season. We have to work on keeping our eyes, our focus on Jesus and rejoice and celebrate Him. Mary, the precious Mother of Jesus, magnified and lifted up the Lord because of the great gift He gave her of Jesus Christ. We should follow her example and magnify the Lord today, and let our spirits rejoice in God our Savior. Have a special prayer, and light a candle in reverence of His name. Make a list of all the Biblical names of Jesus, and write these in a prominent place in our home during this Christmas season, perhaps displaying them on our Christmas tree. At each meal, say a special prayer, paying extra attention to His holiness and bringing extra honor to Him.

Prayer: Lord Jesus, help me to keep my eyes and heart focused on You during this season of Christmas. I rejoice and celebrate You. I magnify the Lord today. Thank You. Amen.

Prayers, Thoughts, Gifts of Joy Today:

DECEMBER 7

"And his mercy is on them that fear him from generation to generation."

-LUKE 1:50

Mary is still talking in this verse, talking about God's mercy, giving us what we don't deserve and sparing us from what we do deserve. God's mercies are new every new day. He has mercy on us and loves and cares for us when we fear (have love, respect, and honor) for Him. Every generation must teach our children and grandchildren to believe in God and to have a holy fear of Him. Then He will bless our nation, our children, our grandchildren, and generations to follow. Christmastime is an excellent time to teach our families to have a love and respect for God. Use this time wisely.

Prayer: God, let me love and worship You in everything I do or say today. Keep my eyes on You. Help me to teach the generation following to respectfully fear (honor, love, respect) You. Thank You. Amen.

Prayers, Thoughts, Gifts of Joy Today:

DECEMBER 8

"And the angel said unto them, Fear not: for, behold, I bring you good tidings of great joy, which shall be to all people."

-LUKE 2:10

G reat joy God gives to us. We should never be afraid because God is on our side. He loves and cares for us through every trial, every problem, and every heartache. He is with us and will be to the end of our days on this earth. God sent Jesus into the world to save us from our sins. We celebrate His coming to earth as a human and making Himself like us for a time. He feels our pain and understands. Because He became a man, He knows what it is like to be a man. In the verse above, it says the angel gives us "good tidings of great joy." Have great joy in this Christmas season because Christ came.

Prayer: Thank You, Jesus, for the great joy You give me. Help me not to fear, but to know You are near. Amen.

Prayers, Thoughts, Gifts of Joy Today:

DECEMBER 9

". . . in thy light shall we see light."

-Psalm 36:9

J esus is the light of the world. He came to a dark world to shine His light on us, and shine the light so that we could see the way to salvation. The Bible refers to Jesus as light, not darkness, many times. To live in His light, His joy, is a blessing God gives us. As we celebrate Christmas this year, as we light candles in our homes, let us look at those lights shining brightly as a reminder of Christ's light in our lives and in our hearts. Light a candle every night during the Christmas season and say a prayer of thanksgiving and praise for Jesus Christ, our Lord and our Savior. This would be a good tradition to start with our family—lighting a candle each night and having a prayer of thanks around the light. We have the power to design the life we want. Start today designing our life around the light of Christ.

". . . design a life of substance, and truly begin to live your dream."

-Les Brown

Prayer: Lord Jesus, let me see Your light and shine Your light to others today in my life. Thank You for lighting my way when I need to see more clearly. Amen.

Prayers, Thoughts, Gifts of Joy Today:

DECEMBER 10

**"The word was made flesh, and dwelt among us,
(and we beheld his glory as of the only begotten
of the Father;) full of grace and truth."**

-JOHN 1:14

Jesus was made flesh when he came to this earth as a human baby. It is hard for us to comprehend that he was all human, yet all God. He chose to come and live here among earthly man, to feel the pain humans feel, to suffer insults, to suffer heartache, and feel agony and rejection on the cross. What a marvelous thing He did for us!

Prayer: Lord, You are full of blessings for us, and I thank You. We celebrate Christmas because You became flesh and lived here on earth. Thank You. Amen.

Prayers, Thoughts, Gifts of Joy Today:

DECEMBER 11

"Glory to God in the highest, and on earth peace, good will toward men."

-LUKE **2:14**

During the Christmas season, we should be especially mindful of giving glory to God. It is a season of peace and good will toward all men. If we harbor bitterness and hatred toward any of our fellow men, we should pray and ask God to help us overcome this. It is hard to get over bitterness toward others when they have hurt us or our loved ones. When we let these feelings simmer and grow in us, roots of anger, resentment, and bitterness will take hold and grow in our lives. Before we know what has happened, our joy and contentment have been overtaken by evil seeds of hatred. We have to constantly be on guard that this doesn't happen to us. We don't want our joy to be stolen. Give God the glory and have peace in our hearts toward all men—even those who have hurt us or done us wrong. Give them and that problem over to God. Cleanse our hearts from anything that might bring anything but glory to God.

Prayer: Glory to You, God! Thank You for Jesus Christ, my Savior. Help me to forgive and have peace with my fellow man today so that You might be glorified. Amen.

Prayers, Thoughts, Gifts of Joy Today:

DECEMBER 12

"He shall be great, and shall be called the Son of the Highest. . . ."

-LUKE **1:32**

F orget about the worries and concerns of this day, this world, and focus instead our heart and mind on Jesus, the Son of the Highest. In this season of celebration of His birth, let us look to Him and be wrapped in His arms of love. He has us. Trust Him. He is there for us at all times, in every situation. He is with us right now, right where we are. Just ask Him to help. Thank Him. Trust Him.

Prayer: Lord Jesus, You are great! Thank You for ALL you have done in my life and will do in the future. Amen.

Prayers, Thoughts, Gifts of Joy Today:

DECEMBER 13

"I am the light of the world . . . ."

-JOHN 8:12

L ight shines in the darkness and directs us, keeps us from stumbling and falling. Jesus came as a light to the world—a light in the darkness for us to see more clearly. He shows us the way to live, directs our path for us with His Word. When we follow Him, we will not stumble around quite so much in the darkness. Candles seem to be a symbol of Christ's light. Light a candle during the Christmas season and think on Christ. Think on His light, shining in and through us. Be His light in a dark world. We are to shine brightly for Jesus today as we go about our usual day. Think before we speak and do. Think joy. Think kindness. Think encouragement. Think helpfulness. Think mercy. Think love.

"Keep your face to the sunshine, and you cannot see the shadow."

-HELEN KELLER

Prayer: Jesus, thank You for Your light, directing my way. Let me follow You even more closely, walking in Your light. Amen.

Prayers, Thoughts, Gifts of Joy Today:

DECEMBER 14

"For God, who commanded the light to shine out of darkness, hath shined in our hearts, to give the light of the knowledge of the glory of God in the face of Jesus Christ."

-2 CORINTHIANS 4:6

God has shined His light into our hearts. Hallelujah! He gives light and hope to our lives. He gives us knowledge of the glory and wonder of God. He sent Jesus, our Christ, into the world to show us the way, the truth, and the light. Let us follow His light today!

"When we sow love, joy grows."

-GERMAN PROVERB

Prayer: Oh Lord, let me follow Your light more closely today. Fill me with Your light, love, and joy. Help me to share these with others. Thank You. Amen.

Prayers, Thoughts, Gifts of Joy Today:

DECEMBER 15

"Let every thing that hath breath praise the Lord. Praise ye the Lord."

-PSALM 150:6

What better time to praise and glorify the Lord than the month we celebrate His birth? Praise Him. Lift Him up. Glorify Him every day. His praise should be on our tongues constantly. He is worthy of our praise and adoration. Praise the Lord for all of His mighty and wondrous works. Praise Him still for the small things He does and for the miracles of life we experience every day. When we pay attention, we will see His hand in everything that is happening around us, from the tiny snow crystals that fall and land on our windowsill to the loveliness and miracle of a newborn baby in our family. "Praise ye the Lord."

Prayer: Today, Lord, I will lift up Your name in praise and adoration. I love You. I worship You. I depend on You. Thank You for every miracle in my life. You are worthy of my praise and adoration. Amen.

Prayers, Thoughts, Gifts of Joy Today:

DECEMBER 16

"That was the true Light, which lighteth every man that cometh into the world."

-JOHN 1:9

The true Light is Jesus Christ. His light, hopefully, will shine through us. Let us shine for Jesus in this dark world today. Let us not hide our light, but rather, sit it up high on a stand and light the world around us. By our fruits—what we do and say—the world will know us. Let our fruit (our actions and deeds) be good for Jesus' sake.

Prayer: "May the words of my mouth and the meditations of my heart be acceptable to You, O Lord." May my words and deeds match my Christian faith and never bring dishonor to You, Christ. Thank You. Amen.

Prayers, Thoughts, Gifts of Joy Today:

DECEMBER 17

"The Lord is my light and my salvation."

-PSALM 27:1

This verse is a blessing, that the Lord is a light and savior to us. We are blessed by Him. Let us bless others in His name as we go about our way today. In this Christmas season, we need to think even more of how we can be a blessing to others and to share Jesus. He has given us so much. We want to become more aware of those around us and think of ways we can be a light in this world to them. We ask the Lord to help us daily to shine His light. Because He has been a salvation to us, so should we shine His light of hope and salvation to others. By being all we can be—and sharing our time, our talents, our energies, our money, our earthly goods, and our love with others—we can shine His light. Look for ways today to shine!

"Behave in a manner consistent with the way you want to feel."

-GLENN VAN EKEREN

Prayer: Lord, help me to share Your light more every day and be ready to help others. Thank You. Amen.

Prayers, Thoughts, Gifts of Joy Today:

DECEMBER 18

"Through the tender mercy of our God; whereby the dayspring from on high hath visited us, to give light to them that sit in darkness and in the shadow of death, to guide our feet into the way of peace."

-LUKE 1:78-79

Dayspring is used in the above verse to describe the dawn, the breaking of light in the morning. The first light of day is a special time. Jesus is the light who has visited us, giving us light in our dark world. We no longer have to fear death because He has given us the promise of eternal life with Him in heaven. There is great hope and a peace in our lives because of this promise. Hope is a wonderful gift from God. When we "sit in darkness" (sadness or gloom) or in the "shadow of death" (facing unknown things, whether they be illness or death of a loved one), He will guide our feet into light and peace.

Prayer: Thank You, God, for sending us light, hope, and peace. Thank You for leading me into Your peace. Amen.

Prayers, Thoughts, Gifts of Joy Today:

December 19

"... light is come into the world. ..."

-John 3:19

Jesus Christ is the light that came into the world. Let us keep His light shining today in all we do and say. Keep Him in the forefront of our mind today as we hurry with our Christmas list of "things to do." Do something for Jesus today. What will we do for Him for Christmas? Take time to pray, read His Word, or lift others up? Pray and care, and give someone else our time? Treat people well today as we go out and about for the sake of Jesus. Think about how we react and respond to others today.

"Laughter is sunshine. It chases winter from the human face."

-Victor Hugo

Prayer: Lord, thank You for my life, for all the blessings You have given me. Let me be aware, notice others' needs, and be willing to take the time to help them. Amen.

Prayers, Thoughts, Gifts of Joy Today:

"O come, let us worship and bow down: let us kneel before the Lord our maker . . ."

-Psalm 95:6

Worship— "Revere, reverence, venerate, pay honor to, adore, praise, glorify, exalt, extol." Worship and adore Him, Christ the Lord, the King of Glory! Let us bow down before Him and realize just who He truly is. He is our maker, our Savior, our Redeemer, Lord, and King! We should be in awe of Him today and every day. When we take our eyes off Him, we can easily lose sight of who He is. This is why it is so important to read His Word and to pray, to keep aware of Him in our lives daily. Stay in continuous contact with Him. That is what He wants.

Prayer: O Lord, I worship and bow down to You today. Let me adore You more. Thank You for the power of prayer in my life. Amen.

Prayers, Thoughts, Gifts of Joy Today:

DECEMBER 21

"I have trusted in thy mercy; my heart shall rejoice in thy salvation."

-PSALM 13:5

We should rejoice and be filled with joy today because of all God has done for us! Oh, life may not be perfect. There may be troubles, problems, illness, tiredness, and brokenness, but remember His mercy and His salvation. He will lift us up, sustain and keep us in His hand. Keep praying. Keep on praying and trust Him to bring us through. Think on the good things in our life right now—the blessings. Write a list of all the things for which we are thankful, and read them aloud in a prayer, thanking God for each one of them. This will encourage and strengthen our hearts. Being thankful brings more joy into our lives. This is the season of joy, so rejoice today.

Prayer: Lord, thank You for all of the many blessings You have given me. I am thankful. I trust in Your mercy and my heart is joyful. Amen.

Prayers, Thoughts, Gifts of Joy Today:

DECEMBER 22

"I will sing unto the Lord, because he hath dealt bountifully with me."

-Psalm 13:6

S ing a song of praise to the Lord today. Rejoice and be filled with joy, for He has us. He has this—whatever this is. We can give our burdens, our worries, and our concerns to God. Trust Him to work this out for the good. Lift Him up in song and thanksgiving today. Thank Him for His loving kindness to us. We are blessed by God, and He has done wonderful things for us. Notice them. Thank Him. An attitude of thankfulness through the Christmas season is the right attitude.

Prayer: Lord, I sing praises to You today. Thank You for all of my many wonderful blessings. Amen.

Prayers, Thoughts, Gifts of Joy Today:

DECEMBER 23

". . . they presented unto him gifts; gold, and frankincense, and myrrh."
-MATTHEW 2:11

What gifts will we give to Jesus for the celebration of His birth? Look into our heart and find a gift for Him to show our love and adoration. Will it be our time, our prayers, our money, or our love? Will we do for others to help honor Him? Whatever our gift is, give it to Him in honor and love—willingly. He is worthy of all we are and all we have. We can look into our hearts and find exactly what we need to do for Jesus, in His honor. Today, find a way in which to honor Him in the way we go about our day. Go with a smile on our face and love in our heart. God will lead us in what to do, whether it be in saying something kind to someone we meet, letting another go in front of us in line at a busy store, paying for a stranger's meal in a restaurant, giving a special gift to a worthy cause, buying clothes or gifts for those less fortunate, or giving our time to an organization doing a good work in Jesus' name.

Prayer: Lord, what do I bring to You today as a gift? You have given me all I have. All I am is Yours. Let me honor You with all my life-all I am, all I say, and all I do. Thank You. Amen.

Prayers, Thoughts, Gifts of Joy Today:

DECEMBER 24

". . . even from everlasting to everlasting, thou art God."

                                            -PSALM 90:2

Always and always, He is God. Revere Him. Think on what He has done for us. Praise His Holy name. Come before Him in praise, thanksgiving, and wonder. Amazing! He is our God. He created us. He loves us and cares about us. He gave us salvation, love, and an always open way into His very presence. That is His gift to us—one of the many. We stand in awe of Him and who He is. Tonight, go outside and just look up into the winter night sky. Breathe in the fresh, crisp air. Breathe in God's love. He is here with us right now, right where we are. Isn't that amazing? Really thank Him.

Prayer: My God and Savior, I thank You. I praise You. I adore You. Amen.

Prayers, Thoughts, Gifts of Joy Today:

DECEMBER 25

"For unto you is born this day, in the city of David a Savior, which is Christ the Lord."
-LUKE 2:11

Oh my, this is mind boggling when we really think about what this means. The very wonder of this miracle to us, this gift to us as His created ones. He became a human. From out of glory in heaven, He chose to become one of His creation, to live among mankind. He is our Savior, Christ the Lord!!! Today, Christmas Day, we should take time out of our busy schedule—our gift giving, our eating, our traveling to visit family or friends—and just think awhile on the miracle of what Christmas really means to us. In the early morning when we rise, stop and say a special prayer of thanks. In the evening, sitting in front of the sparkling tree, take a moment to pray again, maybe read the Christmas birth story aloud and contemplate what was given to us in the person of Jesus Christ.

Prayer: Thank You is not enough to say, Lord, but thank You for giving to mankind the greatest gift of love, Jesus Christ. Amen.

Prayers, Thoughts, Gifts of Joy Today:

DECEMBER 26

"For mine eyes have seen thy salvation."

-LUKE **2:30**

Our salvation is from Jesus Christ. By believing in Him, we have the hope of glory and eternal life. There comes a time in every person's life when we are faced with the decision as to whether to believe in Jesus as Christ or not to believe. If we choose to believe, we pray and ask Him to forgive us our sins and to come into our hearts and lives and live in and through us in this world. We ask Him to lead our lives, to guide us as we live each day. We offer ourselves up to Him as His vessel. When we accept Jesus as our personal Savior, we are accepting who He is and what He is—we are accepting the Bible as His Word and our guidebook for life.

Prayer: Thank You, Jesus, that my eyes have seen You as my salvation. Thank You for coming into my heart and life. Help me to live for You today. Amen.

Prayers, Thoughts, Gifts of Joy Today:

DECEMBER 27

". . . if any man be in Christ, he is a new creature: old things are passed away; behold, all things are become new."

-2 CORINTHIANS 5:17

When we accept Jesus Christ as our Savior and ask Him to forgive us our sins and come into our hearts and life, we start afresh and anew. We start over as a new person. All of our past sins are forgiven and behind us. As we live our lives and time goes by, we have to ask forgiveness for sins, for blessings anew, for God to refresh us, to "restore to us the joy of our salvation," as in Psalm 51:12. Even though we are Christians, that doesn't mean we will never sin again. Keep forgiveness fresh for ourselves and for others. Pray daily to be renewed and refreshed in our walk with the Lord.

Prayer: Thank You, Lord, for my salvation. Help me to live today in renewed love, and when I fail You, let me see it right away and ask for Your forgiveness. Amen.

Prayers, Thoughts, Gifts of Joy Today:

"I called upon the Lord in distress: the Lord answered me, and set me in a large place. The Lord is on my side; I will not fear: what can man do unto me?"

-PSALM 18:5-6

The Lord is on our side! He loves us. He wants only good for us. Call upon Him, pray, and ask for guidance and help in times of distress. He is there for us, always. The Lord has us. What can man do to us? Oh, they might hurt us, even kill us, but if God has us—and He does— then nothing man does has any eternal effect on us. God is in control, not man.

Prayer: Thank you, Lord, for always being with me and being on my side, helping me. I will not fear because You are with me. Amen.

Prayers, Thoughts, Gifts of Joy Today:

DECEMBER 29

". . . rejoice, because your names are written in heaven."

-LUKE 10:20

When we accept Christ as our Savior, ask Him to forgive our sins and to come into our life, our name is written down in the Book of Life in heaven. We should rejoice and be glad, celebrate this over and over. We can have peace, security, and joy because of this fact. When our names are written down, nothing can take that away. God has us with Him for eternity.

Prayer: God, I thank You for coming into my heart, for Your love, forgiveness, and salvation. I am joyful for my name is written by You in heaven. Amen.

Prayers, Thoughts, Gifts of Joy Today:

DECEMBER 30

"The Lord is my strength and song. . . ."
-PSALM 118:14

At the end of another year, let us look to the Lord Jesus Christ to be our strength and our song in the year ahead. We can look ahead with joy in our hearts because of who He is—our Lord and Savior. Draw strength from His Holy Word, strength for today and for all of our tomorrows. Pray, thank Him, trust Him, lean on Him in all we do. We can do whatever lies ahead for us with the help and strength God gives us. We should have bright hope for the future. God is with us always. At the end of a year, I like to write down all the things accomplished in the past year, looking back with great thanks for God's help and answered prayers in life. By doing this, we can see in a tangible way some of the ways in which God has led our lives and blessed us.

Prayer: Lord of strength, power, and might, I come to You today asking for more of Your strength and blessings on my life. Put a song in my heart today. Let me find Your joy and peace. Thank You. Amen.

Prayers, Thoughts, Gifts of Joy Today:

"... behold, I make all things new."

-REVELATION 21:5

Today is the end of a year, yet at midnight, a new beginning will occur—a new year, a new day for us. Remember, God makes all things new! No matter what we have done, He can and will heal, restore, and cleanse when we ask in sincere repentance. He can make our life new, and we can start the new year fresh and joyful. Only Jesus can make us new. Only He can give us true joy, peace, and hope in the year ahead. Pray right now, and ask for His help with everything that is troubling us. He cares and wants to help. He will be there with us through it all. He will "make all things new."

"We have to make the choice to be happy in a particular situation, just as it is."

-NORMAN VINCENT PEALE

Prayer: Lord Jesus, take away this fear, this worry, this anxiety, and lack of faith, and make me new in spirit. Fill me with Your joy and hope right now. I thank You. Amen.

Prayers, Thoughts, Gifts of Joy Today:

GLOSSARY

Encouragement: February 1, February 19, February 20,
              February 23
              March 6, March 19, March 24,
              March 31
              May 1, May 17
              June 13
              July 30
              August 10, August 13

Faith: January 17
Trust   February 11
              March 17, March 23
              April 11, April 19, April 22, April 24,
              April 28, April 29
              May 4, May 7, May 25, May 30
              July 23, July 29
              August 17, August 18, August 20
              September 12, September 24
              October 25, October 29

Fear: January 22, January 27
              February 4, February 28
              March 4, March 11, March 13,
              March 20
              May 15
              June 14, June 28

Fear Continued: September 16, September 19, September 20, September 30

October 24, October 28

November 1, November 2, November 6

December 8, December 28

Grief:
Sorrow
Heartache

February 8, February 9

March 15

May 12, May 19

July 6, July 14, July 26

August 8, August 22

October 3, October 21, October 23, October 26

December 28

Help: January 23, January 24, January 28

February 21

March 2, March 22, March 30

April 7, April 14, April 17

May 2, May 6, May 9

June 22

July 1, July 2, July 8, July 27, July 30

August 1, August 9, August 11, August 26

September 1, September 18, September 29

October 20, October 23

November 18

Hope: January 2

February 6, February 22, February 24

March 1, March 8, March 14
June 7, June 8, June 17
July 5, July 6
August 11, August 15, August 16, August 30
September 2, September 21, September 25,
September 26, September 28
October 3, October 6, October 11, October
22, October 25,
December 26, December 27, December 31

Joy: January 1, January 3-January 10, January 14,
January 16, January 18
February 2, February 25
March 18
April 6, April 8, April 30
May 24, May 27, May 31
June 12, June 16, June 21, June 23, June 25,
June 29
August 5
September 22, September 23
October 4
November 9, November 10, November 22
December 3, December 6, December 8,
December 21, December 29

Peace: January 19, January 21, January 29
February 9, February 27
March 9
April 12, April 18

Peace Continued: May 3, May 22
June 18
July 20
August 12
December 4, December 11,
December 18

Prayer: January 25, January 26
February 18
April 1, April 13, April 18, April 27
June 3, June 4, June 11, June 17
July 3, July 4, July 7, July 11, July 17
August 15, August 19, August 23,
August 25
October 1
November 9, November 16, November 17

Safety: April 4, April 16
Security   May 5, May 8, May 14, May 20,
May 29
June 11, June 24, June 26
July 21, July 25
August 21, August 22, August 26,
August 29, August 31
September 10, September 27
October 10, October 17, October 18,
October 22
November 11
December 1, December 31

Sing: January 13, January 20
February 3, February 10, February 15
March 29
April 2, April 9, April 20, April 21
May 21, May 28
July 28
August 3
September 17
October 7, October 8, October 9
November 18
December 22

Strength: January 9, January 11
February 7, February 14
March 3, March 5, March 12, March 27
April 3, April 15
June 2, June 4
July 10, July 11, July 13, July 18
August 1, August 2, August 9
September 14, September 16, September 17, September 28
October 5, October 14, October 27, October 28
December 30

Success: February 5, February 26
March 25, March 26, March 28
April 10
June 1, June 3, June 10, June 19, June 30

Success Continued:	July 12
	September 9
	October 13, October 29, October 30
	November 8, November 13,
	November 21
Thanks:	January 12
	February 12
	May 13, May 16
	July 17, July 24
	August 4, August 6, August 8, August 23
	September 4, September 5, September
	6, September 7
	October 19
	November 15, November 23,
	November 24, November 27
Trials:	January 6, January 12, January 30
Troubles	February 16, February 29
	March 10
	April 25, April 26
	May 10, May 11
	June 7, June 22
	July 26
	August 22
	September 29
	October 3, October 7, October 21,
	October 23
	December 28

Worry: January 31
February 13
March 16, March 21
April 5, April 23
May 23
June 15
October 24
November 2, November 26,
November 30

Acknowledgements

I was blessed to have so many family and friends encourage and help me with this project. I want to acknowledge and thank my daughters, Karen and Kristi, always, and my sons-in-law, Brian and Jeff. I call on the sons-in-law to help with all technical support and equipment failures, and daughter Karen for her writing expertise. She allows me to bounce ideas off her and call her endlessly with questions. Kristi is my calm and steady encourager.

Thank you also to Joyce Mochrie, owner of "One Last Look," who was again my copy editor and proofreader. She is a god-send, and I have learned to depend on her knowledge and ability and trust her instinct.

Go to sandramansfieldwright.com for more information and to follow my blog.

Made in the USA
Lexington, KY
29 January 2018